15.00

AFRICAN HUNTER

BIG GAME

AFRICAN HUNTER

Baron Bror von Blixen-Finecke

Translated from the Swedish by F. H. Lyon

Peter Capstick, Series Editor

St. Martin's Press
New York

To the Reader:

The editors and publishers of the Peter Capstick Adventure Library faced significant responsibilities in the faithful reprinting of Africa's great hunting books of long ago. Essentially, they saw the need for each text to reflect to the letter the original work, nothing having been added or expunged, if it was to give the reader an authentic view of another age and another world.

In deciding that historical veracity and honesty were the first considerations, they realized that it meant retaining many distasteful racial and ethnic terms to be found in these old classics. The firm of St. Martin's Press, Inc., therefore wishes to make it very clear that it disassociates itself and its employees from the abhorrent racial-ethnic attitudes of the past which may be found in these books.

History is the often unpleasant record of the way things actually were, not the way they should have been. Despite the fact that we have no sympathy with the prejudices of decades past, we feel it better—and indeed, our collective responsibility—not to change the unfortunate facts that were.

—Peter Hathaway Capstick

AFRICAN HUNTER. Copyright © 1986 by Peter Hathaway Capstick. All rights reserved. Printed in the United States of America. No part of this book may be used or reproduced in any manner whatsoever without written permission except in the case of brief quotations embodied in critical articles or reviews. For information, address St. Martin's Press, 175 Fifth Avenue, New York, N.Y. 10010.

Library of Congress Cataloging in Publication Data

Blixen-Finecke, Bror, baron von, 1886–1946.
    African hunter.

    Translation of: Nyama (vilt).
    1. Big game hunting—Africa, Central. I. Title.
SK255.A32B5513   1986   799.2'0967   85-26075
ISBN 0-312-00959-3

10 9 8 7 6 5 4 3

EDITOR'S NOTE TO THE REPRINT EDITION

IT is a hard act to follow when Ernest Hemingway (aye, Himself), on receiving his Nobel Prize in 1954, insisted that Karen Blixen (Isak Dinesen) deserved it far more. This is not, however, the story of Baroness Karen von Blixen-Finecke—the woman who wrote such haunting books as *Out of Africa, Shadows in the Grass,* and *Seven Gothic Tales*—it is rather that of her husband, who was one of the greatest professional hunters in Africa during the period between the end of the First World War and the late 1930s. Although Blixen never authored such as *Out of Africa,* his ghost need not blush at *African Hunter,* which has long been regarded as fine Africana since its translation from Swedish in 1938 by F. H. Lyon.

EDITOR'S NOTE

It is, in my experience, rare for writers to whom falls the high honor of producing personal comments on the works of greater writers not to take every advantage of their position. In the case of Baron Bror von Blixen-Finecke, I really see no point in speaking at length of his youth, his background, and his techniques with big and dangerous game, as he does it so well himself. It's not my job to tell his story before he can do so himself.

If I may have your time as you pour a tall brown one or light your pipe, I should like to make a practical, no-kidding comparison between the days of Blixen when "they slaughtered game" and those of today.

Many people who know little better would call Blixen a "murderer" today or something equally charming and emotionally inaccurate. Kenya stopped hunting entirely in the mid-1970s, which resulted in two certainties: number one, there were no funds to pay a game department to protect game, collect license fees, and keep protective game managers in the field, and number two, the poachers had a field day as there was nobody to stop them. That Jomo Kenyatta's family used the national airline as the main route to the east for ivory and rhino horn did not seem to mean much to those possessed with a "genuine" interest in preservation. The idea was to stop hunting, the essential evil, in any form.

As I was to discover during a promotional tour of Great Britain during 1980, these last four-score years have witnessed a change in general and specific attitudes toward wildlife a good many thousands of miles from Africa. The very people who brought the world the concepts of "fair chase" and "sportsmanship" in their fetal form were—and are today, with noted exceptions—antibloodsport. I have pondered the reasons for this and can only come up with the personal conclusions that hunting is resented as being one of the indolent pastimes of the privileged and/or the nobility, and that sheer "preservationism" is the only answer. Yet surely no wild species is better cared for than the Scottish grouse, which represents a literal market crop as well as vast, local in-season employment. Why? The Kenya reasons of the old hunting days resurface. The grouse are the *real* value of the land that has no other economic worth beyond some grazing and, if the owner is lucky, perhaps the leasing of a good trout burn or even of a salmon river. Again, in Great Britain, shooting as well as fishing pay their own way, if permitted to do so.

EDITOR'S NOTE

Yes, the few die that the thousands may live. Were it not so—at least in Africa, and especially in Kenya, which has the highest human growth rate in the world—there would be nothing left but goats and cattle, of which there is no shortage now.

But before returning to the real object of this commentary, which is Africa and not Britain, one last point: Americans buy well over twenty million hunting licenses each year to support their natural wild areas. Clearly, hunting as an economic tool is vital for ecological balance.

Bror Blixen lived in the great era of East African hunting, and was considered one of the finest of the anointed. Born in 1886, he was the twin son of a Swedish baron and a Danish countess and was raised in opulence, soon acquiring a taste for the hunt. A robust, stocky man of spring-steel nerves and superb marksmanship, Blixen had the rare combination of being an aristocrat and, it would appear, a bit of a bounder to all who knew him.

Blixen had known Karen Dinesen for some years before he became engaged to her in 1912, much to the alarm of her family, who disapproved of the irrepressible Swede. The young couple eventually found their way to Kenya as a direct result of the enthusiastic description given

EDITOR'S NOTE

by one of Bror's uncles, who had just enjoyed a grand safari in British East Africa and who emphasized the economic possibilities of that part of the world.

Karen's family provided the money for a farm near Nairobi where coffee was to be grown. So it was that Karen sailed out in 1913 to join Bror in Mombasa, where they were married, Bror having preceded her in order to attend to the farm transaction and establish a house. He was already well and truly smitten by the charm of that vast country, so different from the world he had left.

It was not long after Blixen and his wife had settled on their farm that he started womanizing. This culminated in Karen becoming infected with syphilis, from which she never recovered. Bror was less than shy with the Masai maidens, among whom the disease was rife. His forays into town and his often wild socializing at the Muthaiga Club, coupled with a legendary indiscipline when it came to money and honoring his debts, soon gave the charming Swede a notorious reputation. To quote Judith Thurman in her magnificent book *Isak Dinesen: The Life of a Storyteller* (St. Martin's Press, New York, 1982), Bror was "one of the most durable, congenial, promiscuous, and prodigal creatures who ever lived."

Blixen and his wife spent a rather strange time

EDITOR'S NOTE

during the First World War. Karen was suspected of being a spy for the Germans, whereas Bror managed to get along very well with the community as a whole, consorting with a host of cronies and dabbling in all kinds of schemes. Known by the African-given name of "the waddler" or *Wahoga* because of his thick-set stature, Blixen became a professional hunter after the end of the war, and succeeded in conducting safaris for some of the great personalities of the day into new areas, where he helped to pioneer the industry. He twice accompanied the Honourable Denys Finch Hatton, son of the thirteenth Earl of Winchilsea and Nottingham, on safari with H.R.H. The Prince of Wales. Blixen knew of the great love affair between Finch Hatton and his wife, but seemed to ignore it. The farm did not prosper for a variety of reasons and the Blixens eventually parted company, Bror devoting all his energy and time (when not dodging his creditors) to hunting. He moved with ease in the most elevated company and gained undying fame for his charm and wild ways as a hunter in East Africa. Finch Hatton, in the meantime, was killed in a private aircraft accident at Voi in 1931. Karen Blixen returned to Denmark soon afterward, never to see Africa again.

EDITOR'S NOTE

After some years, Bror also left Africa in the late thirties for America, where he managed the country estate of an American gentleman of rare wealth for a time. He survived two divorces after his divorce from Karen and finally returned to Sweden, where he died in 1946 as a result of injuries sustained in a car crash. This was a strange end to the seemingly indestructible Blixen. As Judith Thurman noted, he had "a Rasputinlike constitution, which not poison, disease, malaria, war, breaks and gashes of all kinds nor the most violent general wear seemed able to dent." Ernest Hemingway knew Blixen well and it is generally believed that his hero Robert Wilson, the hunter in *The Short and Happy Life of Francis Macomber,* was based on Blixen.

I know not what Bror von Blixen-Finecke's headstone reads. I can only quote the truly poignant words of Karen Blixen who, thirty years after her first safari with Bror in Kenya and despite all the intervening years of ill health and unhappiness, was able to remark to a friend: "If I should wish anything back of my life, it would be to go on safari once again with Bror Blixen."

—PETER HATHAWAY CAPSTICK

CONTENTS

I.	STARTING A FARM	3
II.	GAME LAWS — GAME-PRESERVING — LICENSES	27
III.	BUFFALOES	37
IV.	ELEPHANTS	54
V.	LIONS	80
VI.	"GOOD, DANGEROUS SPORT"	100
VII.	RHINOCEROS AND OTHER GAME	109
VIII.	COOPER	119
IX.	IN CRATERLAND	132
X.	CANNIBALS	144
XI.	PYGMIES	154
XII.	BELIEFS AND SUPERSTITIONS	168
XIII.	"I'M THE PRINCE OF WALES"	178
XIV.	"ONE OF THE TOUGHEST SPORTSMEN"	189
XV.	THE MASAI	205
XVI.	CROCODILES AND HIPPOPOTAMI	217
XVII.	FISHING	226
XVIII.	THE RIVER CONGO AND LAKE CHAD	233

CONTENTS

XIX.	Our Sahara trip	242
XX.	An elephant farm	253
XXI.	Courage and endurance	262
XXII.	Bad luck	270
XXIII.	1914	274
XXIV.	After twenty-three years	280
	Index *follows page*	284

ILLUSTRATIONS

BIG GAME	*frontispiece*
THE AUTHOR AND HIS WIFE	22
A HUNDRED-AND-TWELVE-POUNDER	23
THE AUTHOR AND A LITTLE WAMBOUTI GIRL	38
SIR CHARLES MARKHAM WITH BOBO	39
FOUR ELEPHANTS SHOT ON A SIX DAYS' HUNT	70
HERD OF ELEPHANTS EMERGING FROM A SWAMP	71
"LIONS DON'T CLIMB TREES"	86
LIONS FIND A SHOT ZEBRA	87
CAMERA HUNTERS APPRECIATE THE RHINOCEROS	102
THREE-HORNED RHINOCEROS, SHOT IN 1932	103
CHEETAH WITH ITS PREY	118
NATURE AND ART; RHINOCEROS AND AN AEROPLANE	119
ZEBRAS AT THE TANA RIVER	134
THERE'S DANGER ABOUT	135

ILLUSTRATIONS

Wambouti infantry in the firing line	*166*
Life has left its marks	*167*
Hippos at play	*182*
Ripon falls, the source of the Victoria Nile	*183*
Native fishermen on an African lake	*230*
An alarming charge	*231*
Murcherson's fall, Victoria Nile	*246*
A Sahara fortress	*247*

AFRICAN HUNTER

I. *Starting a Farm*

I CANNOT say how old I was when I had a gun in my hands for the first time, but that my fingers itched to hold a weapon rather than a book is beyond question. I do not think I can be charged with being afraid of hardships — these pages should rather prove the contrary — but I have always stood somewhat in awe of bookwork. Our revered educational institutions, sad to say, could never spur me to the least endeavor to win trophies within their walls: I have had more luck with lions than with school prizes in my day.

The man makes the milieu, and the milieu makes the man, I have read somewhere. I was born — fifty years ago — at Näsbyholm in Skåne, the family estate, where the best shooting in Sweden is to be found. The woods and fields swarm with game, from deer to hares and birds, and the game is not only shot, but preserved. The atmosphere is charged with sporting observations and experiences which cannot fail to stir a boy's imagination, and if the boy is a sportsman by instinct to begin with, his outlook on life is pretty quickly determined. The freedom of the fields and woods, the joy in wandering about at will, without compulsion, and observing wild things and scenery, causes a strange singing of the blood — it is a tune one never forgets, which no school discipline can drive out of one's mind.

For of course I had to go to school, when the time came — at Lund. It was bound to be a fiasco. The daily grind of the classroom cannot fail to be a minor hell for a boy who has grown accustomed to roam about under God's sky without let or hindrance. Masters and pupil parted without tears of regret.

Alnarp. Things went better there. But please do not think the young man turned out a model pupil! On the contrary, I am afraid I was always on the wrong side when there was a difference of opinion as to the solution of any disciplinary problem. But enough! Anyhow, I learned so much about agriculture that they were bold enough to

STARTING A FARM

make me responsible for the tenant farm of Stjärneholm, on the Näsbyholm property. Certainly the result was not bad, and it is not inconceivable that I should have been living in Skåne, a well-to-do farmer, this very day if something rather important had not happened — I got engaged to the girl whom I called Tanne, but whom the whole world was to know many years later as Isak Dinesen, authoress of *Seven Gothic Tales*.

The human imagination is a curious thing. If it is properly fertilized it can shoot up like a fakir's tree in the twinkling of an eye. Tanne knew the trick, and between us we built up in our imagination a future in which everything but the impossible had a place. The promised land which hovered before our eyes was called Africa, and our golden dreams included a large farm, teeming with fine fat cattle.

Nor was it just a castle in the air. Behind our imaginings lay a reality, named Aage Westerholz, an uncle of Tanne's. This excellent man was, among other things, the owner of a rubber plantation in Malaya.

"What would you say to exchanging Stjärneholm for my rubber plantation in Malaya?" he asked 'me one fine day.

It was like asking a horse if he would care for

some oats! I accepted gratefully, without a moment's reflection. At twenty-five one does not search one's conscience anxiously before undertaking a new task; tapping the trees for rubber was no more difficult than cutting the rye when it was ripe, and the rubber market was particularly good at that time. The Malays had an established reputation for willing work and good conduct, so that side of the business caused me no worry either. Our confidence was unbounded.

And then there was the sport. The Perak River swarmed with crocodiles — rewards were actually offered for shooting them — and tigers lurked in the Malayan jungle. This was something better than the Näsbyholm deer!

Uncle Aage smiled at my enthusiasm. No, the shooting in Malaya was not bad, but what was it compared with lion-hunting in East Africa? And the country itself! And the possibilities!

The fact was that another uncle, Count Frijs, had just come home from a big-game hunting expedition in Africa and was so brim-full of impressions of his trip that he could hardly talk of anything else — which was quite understandable. The African highlands around Kilimanjaro and Kenya had so delighted Uncle Mogens that he became almost lyrical. Everyone knows that this sort of thing is infectious. And somehow or other, in our conversations, Malaya withdrew farther and farther into the dim distance.

"A well-run farm in East Africa just now ought to make its owner a millionaire," Mogens Frijs said one day.

"More quickly than a well-run rubber estate in Malaya?" I asked.

"Quite possibly."

"In that case — " I said, and looked at Tanne. She nodded. And so our course was clear. For Penang we read Nairobi; for Malaya, East Africa. We would milk cows and grow coffee instead of cutting slits in the rubber trees, and the only anxiety was how I should be able to put all the money into the bank.

Our optimism was shared by relations and friends, who asked nothing better than to get a corner for themselves and share the ample gains, and after a voluminous correspondence with Africa a farm of seven hundred acres was bought. The gold mine was ours. All we had to do now was to extract the rich ore.

My eagerness to get off to my new activities was of the red-hot variety, but in those days, worse luck, there were no aeroplanes which could run one over from Paris to Kenya in three days. I got on board a boat at Marseilles, which was no slower than most others, but which was naturally quite incapable of keeping pace with my wild imagination. From Port Said, which in those days was nothing but a collection of old wooden hovels, we traveled through the Red Sea and down into the Indian Ocean. Then it was all fresh and exciting to the young traveler — now it is commonplace, the hackneyed theme of so many hundred writers. The reader will be spared any attempt on my part to cast a romantic glamour over that stage of the journey.

But I will tarry a moment at my next destination, the East African harbor town of Mombasa, and the journey from that place to my final goal, Nairobi.

Mombasa! Is there not a flavor of Negro mysticism about the name itself? Something pristine and primitive, which makes one imagine the place as a black Cosmopolis? The reality approximated more nearly to that idea then than it does now, when the town has got its hyper-modern port and a quay at which four up-to-date Atlantic giants can lie comfortably bow to stern. And after the uniformity of the sea one was almost blinded by the swarm of fantastically variegated Oriental costumes.

STARTING A FARM

Here take shape the increasing requirements of the immense East African territory in goods from the other countries of the world. Machines and parts for machinery, agricultural implements and building material, raw products and canned food, textile goods and motor-cars are stacked up in vast quantities to be swiftly passed on farther up country, south, west, and north. And through this same channel, whose water has often been so reddened with the blood of Arabs and Portuguese, flows everything that this part of the fertile African continent gives to the rest of the world in exchange — fruit, corn, hemp, ivory, meat, but, above all, coffee, coffee, coffee. The mathematician is not yet born who could express in figures the number of bags of coffee which have disappeared at these wharves into the cargo boats' gaping jaws, to be passed on to old wives' coffee-pots.

The port and town teem with people. They did so of old and do so still, though, of course, the tempo is continually accelerated. The centuries go side by side. The private car — and there are perhaps more private cars to be seen in Mombasa than in most other civilized towns in the tropics — has to pull up sharply to avoid a black man singing as he carries his load on his head, as he did a hundred years ago. The women brighten with their gaily colored clothes the avenues shaded by enormous mango trees and jostle with their burdens among people of every color, from blackest ebony to palest orange. Along the creek that leads to Kilindini, the modern port, thousand-year-old banyan trees stand, and among them lie the ruins of old Portuguese forts and bastions.

There is a continuous play of contrasts in this strange Mombasa, which so fascinatingly combines the sophisticated and the naïve. Mombasa is built on a coral island. Its streets are always crowded with people unable to read or write, but out on the point by the lighthouse is the golf club, with perhaps the most picturesque course in the world, and not far off the Governor's palace is washed by the waves of the Indian Ocean. The sand lies gleaming white in the tropical sun, beneath the menacing darkness of the lava cliffs. Black and white — the city of sharp contrasts.

The train journey between Mombasa and Nairobi is a matter of eighteen hours. You get into the train at four in the afternoon and arrive at ten next morning. For the first bit one can give oneself up with a quiet mind to the pleasures of the table in the dining-car, and drink a bottle of African Burgundy, which is not so bad by any means, for the scenery is not worth looking at — dreary bush which can give no pleasure to anyone. Nor need one's night's rest in the sleeping-car be disturbed; but at the break of dawn you must be on your legs with eyes wide open! Kilimanjaro! The greatest of Arabian poets has written his most superb, his most heaven-sent poem about Kilimanjaro's snow-peaks drenched in crimson by the sunrise; and he could have been inspired by something worse. The sight is one of those which, once seen, are ever present to the eye.

The railway follows the old caravan road from the coast into darkest Africa, which has been worn by the naked soles of so many million slaves and about which thousands of battles have been fought between Arab traders and Masai warriors.

The train hurries on, the wheels rattling over the rails. Some time ago we crossed the river Athi with its sluggish, brownish-yellow water. Malaria mosquitoes swarmed thick over its faintly rippled surface; on its low banks and at the water's edge crocodiles lay on the watch, as motionless as stranded logs.

With all respect to the scenery, there is something that is bound to make an even greater impression on the traveler — the fauna. One simply cannot believe one's eyes. The train plows its way forward across the plain between whole regiments of giraffes, gnu, antelopes, graceful gazelles (Grant's and Thomson's), ostriches, and zebras. The abundance of wild life which can be seen at close quarters from the train in the early morning is unequaled anywhere in the world. Only a few hundred yards to the southward a big herd of elephants is galloping along, and among them a rhinoceros. Even the naked eye can detect the hyena stealing home to the river-bed after his nocturnal hunting to enjoy his rest during the daylight hours.

And not one of all these animals takes the least notice of the smoking, puffing engine and the rolling cars. The whole performance does not concern them. Every one of them has his own affairs to look after and to think about — let that odd, evil-smelling reptile that is called a train wriggle along as best it can!

Opposite to me in my car on one trip sat a gentleman who did not seem to be very much at home in Africa. He looked longingly at his gun-case, which lay in the rack. Then he looked at me and shook his head with a smile.

"Well," he said, " we'd better keep our fingers to ourselves."

And we certainly had. The whole of this immense steppe, the Athi plain, is a part of the southern game reserve, in which shooting is forbidden. When anything is forbidden in Africa one does best to keep one's distance or heavy fines are inflicted, and are collected with a determination to which one cannot but take off one's hat, if any.

Nairobi in 1913 was more like an empty old anchovy tin than anything else. I cannot exactly say that the town and I fell in love with each other at first sight, even if I was received in the kindliest manner by, among others, the multimillionaire MacMillan, who then reigned over a wide demesne in East Africa. He was a fine fellow, MacMillan, with a full and eventful life behind him — and a tragic death at Monte Carlo awaiting him. But his ashes returned to the regions he loved more than anything else on earth; he lies buried in Donya Sabuk, Buffalo Mountain, a tomb which exactly suits him. My contact with him was through the direct mediation of his friend, the Swedish engineer Åke Sjögren, who threw open his house to me with great kindness and hospitality.

But the town itself, as I have already hinted, was not worth a star in Baedeker. The houses were a collection of scattered, rather shabby tin boxes, among which goats, fowls, and all kinds of other domestic animals led a pleasant rustic life. Where that fashionable street, the present Sixth Avenue, stands there were in those days only isolated huts, and where the gentleman of today turns his Packard into the hyper-modern Government Road, he can scarcely imagine what it was like twenty years ago: an undrained, dirty, clayey cattle track between two lines of giant eucalyptus trees.

But after all, what did it matter? If the place suggested a gold-diggers' camp rather than a town, I had no objection. I was after gold, not smart hotels.

But it was not long before I discovered that the gold I was seeking could not be made out of stockbreeding. Things notoriously look rather different at close quarters and at a distance. Gold meant coffee. Coffee-growing was the only thing which had any future; the world was crying out for coffee from Kenya. I therefore sold my seven hundred acres and bought instead from Mr. Sjögren the Swedo-African Coffee Co., owning 4,500 acres near Nairobi and about the same area near Eldoret.

Now the real difficulties began. It is not enough to have a boat; it must also be made to move in the direction one wishes. I needed the help of seven hundred pairs of black hands, and thought, with a twinge of melancholy, how easy it was to get labor in Sweden — an advertisement in some paper, and the thing was done. In Africa I had to set to and equip a regular small expedition and prepare for a safari of several weeks to visit the various chiefs. I had to induce them by appropriate methods — bribes and fair words — to order their subjects to join my expedition and accept work on my coffee plantation.

My first encounter with the black mentality, as represented by the chiefs in question, was not of the most agreeable kind — to clothe a bitter truth in polite language. A promise given in the evening (of course after the necessary *douceur*) was retracted in the morning. Once I had succeeded in raising three hundred natives, to find next morning that half of them had bolted. How can such things happen? Well, a great deal depends on the respect the natives have for the chief who has bidden them enter the white men's service; if their respect for him is at all shaky, the whole crowd may make tracks during the night. But it may also happen that the wily chief has conveyed to them that the whole ceremony of accepting employment is simply a piece of play-acting, with no other object than to allow the gifts made to him to remain in his possession.

Not many hours had passed before I discovered that the most important item in the equipment of the expedition was neither weapons nor draft animals, but angelic patience on the part of the leader. To show any sign of the rage that boiled in my breast would only have made the situation a great deal worse. If ever I had the chance of practicing the art of clenching the fist in the breeches pocket, it was certainly then.

I quote a few extracts from my diary:

" We drove across immense plains of burned grass, through huge stretches of papyrus; it is as dead and desolate as I picture a moon landscape to be. Now and then a signpost crops up at a cross-road as a faint reminder of civilization and fellow-men, but not a living creature is to be seen. Gradually the country became more pleasant, and about eleven o'clock we passed the Blue Post Hotel, by a roaring stream and a thundering waterfall. It has an imposing name, but is really a much more modest place than it sounds — the hotel consists of a number of primitive huts, in which travelers are lodged, and he who has seen Trollhättan at its best dismisses the waterfall with a pitying smile.

" At one o'clock we drove up to Fort Hall, a small camp, the station of the district commissioner and his fifty native soldiers, who are responsible for the maintenance of order. There is a hospital here too, with a European doctor and nurse, and the fact that all the five Europeans in the community are in the hospital with malarial fever suggests that this is a wise precaution. It seems to be a peculiarly unhealthy region.

"I went straight to the commissioner, but received from him the grievous intelligence that no labor for the plantation was to be had. If we would make ourselves comfortable for four or five days, however, perhaps he could provide the twenty porters we needed to get on to the next halting-place. Lunch — biscuits and jam — was eaten in gloomy silence.

"But I got up at five next morning to try to settle the porter problem for myself, and the early bird caught, not the worm, but seventeen blacks who were willing to join us as porters. The tents were soon struck and packed, but we found that however heavy the burdens we made our black friends carry, we should have to leave a good deal behind.

"Fort Hall is just a rock surrounded by deep valleys; the scenery is desolate and wild; only in the river valleys is there a flash of green. The grass plains lie burned and black for miles round, and the trees have shed their leaves. We followed well-trodden paths through the dreary landscape and met many natives on the road, for this is the great highway down to Nairobi. At three o'clock we reached our first camping-ground, and there we succeeded in getting three men who consented to go and fetch the baggage we had left behind at Fort Hall.

"While waiting for this we encamped by a little river, where I found fresh hippopotamus spoor in the sand. We saw nothing of the animal itself — I had to content myself with shooting one or two guinea-fowl for our dinner; it is astonishing how much lead they will carry. I don't think I killed a single bird that I did not hit plumb in the head.

"The next dawn brought the same difficulties; the seventeen boys could not carry all the baggage, and only after a time-wasting search did we get hold of three women who could be persuaded to carry for us that day. At twelve o'clock we rested by the river Tana, where I shot a zebra to provide our blacks with meat. But there is no such thing as gratitude. When I came back with my booty I was met with the news that all our porters had cleared out without so much as a 'by your leave.'

"Now we were in a regular hole. Porters must be obtained at all costs if the whole expedition's equipment was not to be lost; it was no longer labor for the plantation we were looking for, but just twenty wretched porters to enable us to get on.

"A message was sent to the leading chief in the district, but when at long last the messenger returned he could only report that the chief was with another white man in a buffalo swamp a day's march off, and without his permission I could get no porters. So we must arm ourselves with patience for another three days at least.

"One consolation in our sorrows is that we have tumbled upon a camp-site which has many advantages and which affords excellent opportunities for good and exciting sport. The evening is glorious, the air cool without being cold, and the moon is superbly mirrored in the mighty Tana. Far away across the plains and high up in the mountains gleam the fires from burning grass. Illuminated sections of the horizon remind one of distant towns and villages, and, amid these desolate spaces, I suddenly feel myself surrounded by living communities holding a gay evening festival — another kind of desert mirage. . . ."

After a few days' successful shooting round our camp, a messenger from the chief appeared at last with the news that porters would be placed at our disposal that very day. The chief's right-hand man had promised to send them before evening.

" Can I count on it? " I asked.

" Oh, yes, *bwana*, most certainly," the messenger replied, and turned up the whites of his eyes by way of further assurance.

The sun set — no porters. The night came with peace and coolness, but with no blacks.

In the gray of dawn I determined to go to the chief myself and try to find out how the matter stood. He received me with the greatest civility and explained that unforeseen events had unhappily prevented him from sending the men the day before, but that now it would really be done. He would have the honor of returning my visit a little later in the day, and then the porters would come. The chief came all right, and was offered food and drink and received a knife as a present, but nothing was heard of any porters.

Late in the evening, however, the chief's right-hand man appeared, and with him our hopes returned. Unfortunately there had been a further hitch, but now — at last — it was plain sailing. The porters had been selected, every one of them, and had received definite orders to present themselves at our camp the following morning half an hour after dawn, in a body, under the command of a reliable man.

"I've run all the way to be able to give you this good news, *bwana*," the right-hand man declared, licking his thick lips.

Relieved and full of hope, I had food set before the fellow, and so plausible was his behavior that next morning — before the sun had risen — I had the tents struck and packed, so that everything should be ready when the troop of porters fell in.

We waited and waited. We vied with one another, D. and I, in calling down wrath and curses on the heads of all lying African Negroes. Indeed D., one of the white members of the expedition, was

STARTING A FARM

boiling with rage and making suggestions, each more gruesome than the last, for avenging ourselves on the chief and his right-hand man. No use, my boy! We should only get into a worse mess than we were in already and further diminish our prospects of securing men.

No, there was nothing for it but to seek a new market and let that chief and his African promises go to the deuce. D. and I decided to go alone and endeavor to reach a place named Embu, about twenty-five miles farther on, and try our luck there. Embu had a comparatively large population, and it would be odd if we could not raise the necessary number of porters there — and perhaps labor for the plantation too.

That cursed time of waiting lasted till three o'clock, but as soon as we had made our decision we stirred our stumps. We kept up the pace till ten in the evening, when we reached an Indian shop and asked for a night's lodging. A stable was indicated to us, and we made ourselves as comfortable there as possible. Deep and sweet sleep till dawn, when we continued our journey after a pleasant bathe in the river. We reached Embu soon after nine in the morning, and I there learned to my delight that a man named Tudor Owen was the district commissioner.

" Now you'll see that our troubles are over," I said consolingly to D.

" What do you mean? "

" Tudor is a friend of mine and a good fellow. I've met him in Nairobi. If he can't get us the men we want, nobody can. If I had only had an idea that he was district commissioner here! "

But better late than never, and an hour or two later I had got hold of Tudor. He was delighted to see us and put both his house and his larder at our disposal. His goodwill was absolutely unbounded, but when he heard what my business actually was, his face clouded.

" Of course I'll do what I can to help you," he promised, " but it's not easy to get labor in these parts. The chief who rules over our blacks round about here is called Kater, and he isn't a very reliable sort of fellow."

" Thanks, I've been there before," I replied, not without a tinge of bitterness.

" Wait a moment, Blixen! There's a big trial here in three days, which will collect crowds of people, and till that is over you can't get a single man, for they all have to be at the trial. But afterwards it might be possible to get round Kater by suitable means. . . ."

" And when will the trial be over? "

THE AUTHOR AND HIS WIFE

A HUNDRED-AND-TWELVE-POUNDER

STARTING A FARM

" In a week or so."

" Or so " may mean another two or three weeks, and a week in Africa is about the same as an hour in Europe. D. and I discussed the situation and came to the conclusion that the only thing we could do was to " wait and see." We got porters enough to do the twenty-five miles' march to our last camping-ground and fetch the things we had left there, and then we pitched camp by the river, half an hour outside Embu, to await the end of the trial.

In the meantime we went buffalo-shooting. The country is broken and rather bare, and the grass is burned, so the buffaloes keep to the valleys, whose vegetation to a very large extent has escaped the devastating fire. We had better luck with the buffaloes than with the porters, and were able to add some fine horns to our collection of trophies.

But our shooting did not make us neglect the negotiations with the chiefs in the country round, and one fine morning I was surprised to find sixty-six men drawn up outside the camp, ready to accompany us to the plantation. Just at that time I managed to squeeze another hundred men out of a " labor agent," and D. went off to the plantation with this respectable skeleton of a labor corps to get the clearing work started.

At last the trial was over. Tudor passed the

word to me that the time had now come to begin to talk sense to King Kater, and that potentate seemed to enter into our plans at once. Of course, you can have as many men as you want — five hundred, a thousand; you've only to say the word! I was modest, and contented myself with four hundred. Even if I allowed for a certain percentage of desertions, that ought to be enough, if D. had arrived with his men.

King Kater, Tudor, and I spent a cheery evening together, ate and drank and enjoyed ourselves in a spirit of pleasant mutual understanding. Of course I was especially delighted to feel that the cursed labor problem was solved at last after so much trouble, and I saw in my mind's eye the coffee bushes on my plantation sticking their scrubby tufts up through the soil.

"I should like to see your face tomorrow morning when you stick your head out of the tent door," King Kater said to me genially. "It can't help beaming with delight at the sight of so many fine, strong fellows!"

"Good man!" I burst out, somewhat touched. "Let's drink another glass of beer together!"

We drank another glass, and another, and by and by I went home to my camp. And next morning I thrust my head out of the tent door full of eager expectation. It was as silent and still and desolate as on the day of the Creation. Not a sign of King Kater's four hundred fine fellows. I really wish he had been able to see my radiant face.

Late in the afternoon I went to see him and was received as cordially and amiably as the day before. But now I was angry.

"Stop your talk," I said curtly. "You've cheated me. I haven't got any men. You're a liar."

A sunny smile spread over Kater's face. With what pleasure he had been looking forward to my visit! — for he had guessed that I should honor him in this way. But that was not the only reason why he had neglected to send the men; it had proved impossible at such short notice to collect some of the picked men he had intended for me, and that was why he had postponed sending the contingent. What did a day more or less matter, when such a fine body of men was being collected?

"Then you'll send them tomorrow?" I asked.

Oh, yes! Without fail. It was as certain as the sunrise.

Need I say that no men came the next day either? I went to Tudor.

"You must help me to put the screw on that mealy-mouthed rascal," I said. "I'm not going to put up with this sort of thing."

" What do you want me to do? " asked Tudor. " My Government won't have any trouble with the natives."

" You have the power," I said. " And power notoriously exists to be abused."

Tudor shook his head thoughtfully. Anyhow, the end of the matter was that he agreed to support me in giving King Kater a bit of a fright, and that worked — fifty per cent at least. The next morning I had two hundred men; not a picked lot, worse luck, but good enough.

And so we went off to the plantation.

The soil was cleared. The coffee fields were marked out. The cultivator's hopes swelled in my breast.

Summer went and autumn came — the autumn of 1914.

The war. The price market was chaotic, communications were chaotic. Difficulty upon difficulty arose. The plantation had to be sold — my home was broken up.

I stood there in the forest empty-handed. But I still had my sporting rifle.

II. *Game Laws — Game-Preserving — Licenses*

SHOOTING in Africa does not just mean taking one's gun down from a nail and then going out and blazing away. Game-preservation in Africa is nowadays no empty phrase, but an exceedingly live reality. Game is protected by so many laws and regulations, and their observation so elaborately and strictly enforced, that the authorities have an absolutely effective control over the increase or diminution of the various species. But it is not only the penalties that keeps eager sportsmen in check — to offend against the game laws is considered ungentlemanly.

The supreme authority in matters of game-preservation is the Game Department, whose headquarters for Kenya are at Nairobi, under the game warden, who is in unbroken contact with his subordinates in the various districts. Every district has its assistant game warden, and under him native game rangers to ensure the observance of the game laws in their districts. These are an imposing collection of black gentlemen in uniform, who may turn up pretty well anywhere and politely but firmly ask the sportsman for proof that he has a proper shooting license.

There are a number of different sorts of license, and the cost of them varies, as is right and proper, in accordance with the nature and scope of the permission to shoot. You can get a license for a fortnight for $75, but this does not include either rhinoceros or elephant; and a man who is content to shoot only birds need not pay more than fifteen shillings. Special privileges, too, are accorded to those who are shooting on behalf of some museum; moreover, the Game Department at Nairobi, on special representations being made to it, can make exceptions and concede price reductions on the various licenses if there is any reason for this being done.

The visitor from abroad who is hunting for his own pleasure must be ready to pay £75 for his

GAME LAWS — GAME-PRESERVING — LICENSES

license, and on this document a list is given of what he may kill. A few lions are generally included in the program, but for elephants he must pay a special fee, £25 for the first and £50 for the second. This expenditure on the sportsman's part has been intentionally fixed at such a level that a profit cannot be made on ivory-hunting — though if the hunter is in luck and the animal's tusks unusually heavy a profit can certainly be made, since the price of ivory is seldom below 10$s.$ a pound and the weight of a pair of tusks can sometimes exceed 220 lb. But for the big-game hunter the sport is the main thing.

A license costing £75 entitles the possessor to "hunt, shoot, or capture" the following animals within the State demesnes:

Lion — but only two in the Masai reserve . .	4
Cheetah	1
Hippopotamus (in Lakes Naivasha, Elementeita, and Nakuru, but only with special permission of the Governor) . . .	2
Buffalo — except within certain specified areas	6
Common zebra	20
Grevy's zebra — but only one specimen south of Northern Uaso Nyiro	6
Eland	2

Greater kudu — buck only, and within the following areas:
    (*a*) Turkana province;
    (*b*) Northern Frontier province, but not within 30 miles' radius from Marsabit Post 1
Lesser kudu 6
Bongo — but only one specimen round Aberdare and Kinangop 2
Sable antelope 1
Roan antelope — but not in the Masai reserve and Southern Kavirondo 1
Wildebeest (gnu) — but only four outside the Masai reserve 20
Waterbuck, *Kobus defassa* 2
Waterbuck, *Kobus ellipsiprymnus* . . . 2
Oryx, beisa 6
Oryx, fringe-eared 4
Topi — but not on the Uasin Gishu plateau . 6
Hartebeest, Coke's 10
Hartebeest, Jackson's — but not on the Uasin Gishu plateau 1
Hartebeest — other species 1
Hunter's antelope — but only west of the Burma-Luma road 1
Sitatunga 1
Impala — but not round Kisumu and Lake Naivasha 5

GAME LAWS — GAME-PRESERVING — LICENSES

Bushbuck	20
Reedbuck, Bohor	10
Reedbuck, Chandler's	2
Grant's gazelle	10
but not more specimens than stated below in the following districts:	
(*a*) Northern Frontier province	10
(*b*) Turkana province	8
(*c*) Masai reserve and Nyanza province, in all	4
(*d*) Kikuyu, Nakuru, and Ukamba provinces, in all	4
(*e*) Coast province, excluding Voi district	2
(*f*) Voi district	4
Peter's gazelle	2
Thomson's gazelle	20
Gerenuk (giraffe antelope) — but only two specimens outside the Northern Frontier province	8
Klippspringer	2
Steinbuck (grass antelope)	4
Oribi, Haggard's	4
Oribi, Kenya	1
Oribi, other species, in all	10
Duikers, all species, in all	20
Dik-dik, all species, in all	20
Dwarf antelope	6

Guereza monkey (colobus)	3
Blue monkey	3
Leopard	unlimited number

The owner of one of these licenses has the right to obtain a special license for elephant, rhinoceros, giraffe, and ostrich.

The cost of a hunting expedition to Africa, according to the African Guides tariff, is as follows — including the journey out and home, equipment etc.:

Lorry safari

		£
For one person	for one month	375
ditto	for two months	450
ditto	for three months	550
For two persons	for one month	550
ditto	for two months	650
ditto	for three months	725

To these sums should be added the cost of a white hunter, amounting to between £20 and £25 per month, according to the safari leader's experience and reputation, and of a license, costing from £25 to £75.

"Mule safari" and "ox-cart safari" are cheaper, costing £300 for one person for one month, plus white hunter and license.

GAME LAWS — GAME-PRESERVING — LICENSES

For hunters living in the country the license is cheaper. I pay £10 for my shooting permit, which lasts a year, and he who is fortunate enough to own private preserves may shoot on them for a still lower fee. The natives hunt to this very day with spear and bow and arrows, and often use arrows poisoned with poison of vegetable origin or obtained from putrid meat. Cases of poaching occur now and then, too, despite the close supervision. But if any poor sinner is caught he has to work off his fines, and it is an experience that is not easily forgotten.

The flexible, unremitting supervision is one of the most admirable characteristics of the vast organization which the necessity of preventing the destruction of wild life in Africa has brought into being. St. Bureaucratius is an unknown person in the Game Department. A careful watch is kept on the numbers of the different species of the game, nor is it the department's sole duty to see that these do not sink below a fixed minimum. As soon as any report is received of damage done to property or cattle by the appearance of lions or elephants in such numbers as to be a nuisance, the Game Department organizes an expedition which quickly effects the desired reduction, while the immense sanctuaries in which all hunting is absolutely forbidden

— in Kenya alone, for example, there are two vast game preserves — are a guarantee that extermination need not be feared. All sales of skins and meat are supervised; a breach of the regulations is punished by the withdrawal of the license for three years and fines up to £200.

In 1935 alone, as many as over three thousand elephants were shot in Kenya, Tanganyika, and Uganda simply to protect the natives' banana plantations and cornfields. And if one amuses oneself by going through the African elephant statistics for the past fifteen years, the sales figures for ivory bear astonishing testimony to the scale on which elephants have been killed without any risk of the species diminishing in numbers.

It must not be thought that any white sportsman, for a sum paid, can put himself at the head of a big-game expedition and set forth into the wilds. For this a special license is required; the Game Department examines the application very closely and can refuse it without giving any reason, which, indeed, happens fairly often. These white hunters' licenses are cheap, costing only £1, so that the strictness with which applications are investigated has no economic basis; it is due rather to the insistence on certain personal guarantees that the safari leader is really competent. The

GAME LAWS — GAME-PRESERVING — LICENSES

members of the party may at any time be exposed to danger to life and limb. Moreover, to the leadership of an expedition certain responsibilities are attached which the authorities will only lay upon a person in whom they have confidence; among the leader's obligations are the keeping of a special hunting diary for statistical purposes, which has to be submitted to the Game Department.

When the license has been secured, provisions have to be considered; and here the good old rule comes in that it is wisest not to think of what one must have with one, but what one can do without. Meat, of course, is obtained by shooting, but it is advisable to take a supply of rice, potatoes, and green vegetables. The less one takes in the way of luxuries, the better, as a rule, is the bag. Water must be sought in the field, but a filter is part of the necessary outfit. I have gone hunting with people who have been more insistent on having an ice-box with them than a gun and whose only idea was to take a luxuriously furnished marquee, but there was no gain either in the way of sport or real comfort — rather the opposite.

As to weapons, opinions differ. All kinds of automatic rifles are forbidden, but it is a matter of taste whether one uses a magazine rifle or a double-barreled rifle. The man who wishes to be prepared for all eventualities will do best to take three guns with him — a 6 to 8 mm. Mauser for antelopes and buck, a large-caliber .450 No. 2, for example, for larger and more dangerous animals, and an ordinary double-barreled gun for birds.

But it is at least as important to have first-rate glasses. I can recommend a 7×50 Zeiss. And then the camera — above all, the camera! In the last five or ten years rifle-shooting has given place more and more to camera-shooting, for which nothing but good can be said. For my own part, I must admit that I am one of those who decidedly prefer a good animal photograph of living game to the finest skin on the floor or horns on the wall. A successful photograph demands of the individual much finer sporting qualities than a gun-shot, better nerves, greater patience and endurance. There are many excellent movie cameras nowadays, and films can be developed in Nairobi, which reduces climatic risk to a minimum; but an extra telescopic lens is advisable, for neither the king of beasts nor his vassals are particularly fond of " close-ups."

III. *Buffaloes*

It was December. My friend T. and I had pitched camp on a little tributary of the river Tana, from which fresh buffalo spoor had been reported. T. had a slight attack of malaria, but nevertheless decided to carry out a plan we had arranged previously — to explore the steppe down towards the Tana on parallel lines; as soon as one of us came upon a buffalo he was to send a messenger to let the other know. The country here consists of vast undulating ridges, with solitary thorn trees scattered here and there in the hollows, but otherwise no vegetation but grass, grass, grass as far as the eye can see, huge billowy stretches of grass into which one sinks to the waist and which are very tiring to walk through.

I had already crossed two ridges without seeing the least sign of a buffalo spoor; my legs were getting heavier and heavier in the grass, and the heat of the sun was beginning to be uncomfortable. Was it worth while to go any farther? But three is a lucky number, and as I had managed two ridges I could doubtless achieve the third as well.

Just when I was close to the top of my third ridge, I discovered that I was practically in the midst of a huge herd of buffaloes, a single black mass as far as I could see — the nearest animals scarcely a hundred yards from me. They drew still closer together — I was reminded of lancers closing their ranks to charge — and before they could make the decision they were evidently considering, looking fiercely the while at the solitary man, I raised my rifle and fired at the first bull I could see. The effect was instantaneous; the whole of the rest of the herd turned right about and disappeared down into the valley behind a huge cloud of dust.

But the buffalo I had fired at stood there motionless; he had crept out of the crowd like an avenging specter. There were a few seconds of acute tension. Of course I was ready to fire if he attacked, and he made a feeble effort to do so, but only for a few faltering steps. The giant was done

THE AUTHOR AND A LITTLE WAMBOUTI GIRL

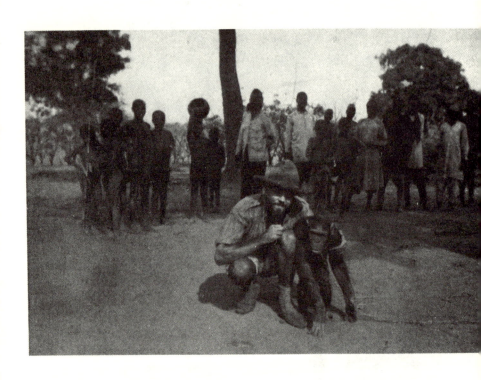

SIR CHARLES MARKHAM WITH BOBO

BUFFALOES

for; he tottered and fell — a few rattling breaths, and life had fled.

I sent the promised messenger to report to T., and two more of my black fellow-hunters to follow the tracks of the fleeing herd, while the rest helped to skin the buffalo and cut up the flesh, which would come in very handy for us. When this was finished, it was about one, but just at that moment the two scouts returned and reported that the herd had halted in a depression about six miles away. My experience told me that it was hardly probable that the beasts would stir until after four o'clock, when the sun had begun to go down, so I took the news quietly. I wanted to wait until T. had arrived.

As soon as he came we started, and although he was not in the best fettle, he struggled on tenaciously for two hours; but just as we had caught sight of the herd of buffaloes he had to give in. Perfectly maddening, but there is no arguing with malaria. But wait! The situation perhaps contained a possibility. If I made an encircling movement with my boys and attacked the buffaloes from the other side, T. would probably get a chance at a shot from the place under a thorn tree where his strength had failed him and towards which we would try to steer some of the herd.

The flanking movement took us some time, and

as soon as we came near the beasts they perceived us. But, curiously enough, they took no further notice of us. Some of them gazed at us quietly, while the great majority lay still on the ground. We for our part were also able to survey the situation at our leisure. I estimated the number of the animals at 350, more rather than fewer. We began to move slowly towards them from a distance of about four hundred yards, with the result that some of the beasts which were lying down got up slowly. A bull with very big horns moved out towards one wing of the herd.

My rifle slid up to my shoulder and the bullet flew towards the big-horned bull's shoulder. Pretty sure that I had hit him clean, I waited to see him fall to the ground dead and the rest of the herd react in the same way as earlier in the day — make a bolt towards the place where T. stood.

But nothing of the sort happened. Big-horns jumped high into the air and set off at a furious gallop towards a small depression to my right. I was following the animal with my eyes, a little surprised at the maneuver, when my gun-bearer, Abdulla, suddenly plucked at my coat to call my attention to what the rest of the buffaloes were doing. They had evidently no intention of repeating the tactics of the morning. As if acting on a word of command, the whole herd had fallen into line, head to head, horn to horn. I can assure the reader that it was a pretty menacing sight, and that there could be no doubt that a mass attack was impending.

There could be no question of resistance. It was not a case of ten to one, but 350 to two, and even if I had had a modern machine-gun at my disposal we should have come off worst. To take to our heels and run for dear life was of no use either; the only consequence would have been that we should have had the whole multitude upon us the next second. The only way of salvation seemed to be to try a slow movement to our right rear, and so avoid the left flank of the buffaloes' front. We put the idea into action at once. But we had hardly taken a step before a silent buffalo command set the column in motion, and the enemy's pace was exactly the same as our own — at first. It looked as if they had seen through our plan immediately, for the left flank showed no inclination to let us slip past. And there was no tree anywhere near to save us, not even the smallest bush by way of cover.

And suddenly the enemy quickened their pace. Certain or almost certain death was swiftly approaching. But love of life creates inspiration; I suddenly thought of the river-bed in which the wounded bull had instinctively sought shelter. Our prospect of getting there before the buffaloes was not great, but it was our only chance. I put on top speed — and a bit more — with Abdulla close at my heels. I exerted every ounce of strength, but it was a terrifyingly long way to the river, and behind us the herd was thundering along.

I looked round. Swiftly as we were running, the distance between pursuers and pursued had diminished, and terribly quickly — now it was scarcely a hundred yards. Long before we could reach the river-bed we should be trampled down and reduced to unrecognizable pulp. Let us sell our lives as dearly as possible!

"Stop, Abdulla!" I cried.

It all happened in a few seconds, but they seemed like minutes — hours. The cloud rolled forward, the thunder grew louder, and out of the cloud the reflection of the sun on the polished horns gleamed like flashes of lightning. At about five yards' range I fired at the buffalo which was rushing straight at me. The animal tottered and fell. The buffaloes on each side of it shied and leaped sideways. A gap was formed in the assault column, and next second the avalanche of buffaloes rushed past, the thunder rolled on, the cloud of dust was wafted slowly away

BUFFALOES

on the wind, and before us lay a cow buffalo in a pool of blood.

Abdulla showed his double row of white teeth, went up to the dead buffalo, and looked at it impassively, as if nothing had happened.

" Fate did not mean us to die this time," he said quietly. So no more words were wasted over that trifling incident.

It appeared later that Fate had quite other plans for Abdulla. The shoulders which carried my rifle so faithfully on many long and hard marches now wear a smart gold-braided coat, and his bare feet no longer sprint for dear life over plains and along jungle tracks, but move with dignified, self-confident gait in Government House, Nairobi.

Abdulla has become butler to Great Britain's highest representative in this part of the globe. But he has my blessing.

There are people who have been hunting in Africa for twenty or thirty years without setting eyes on a lion, and if I parenthetically declare that it is their own fault, I do so with a full sense of responsibility. The man who knows how and when and where to go need never wait more than two or three days for a tête-à-tête with the king of beasts. As for buffaloes, not even the unluckiest sportsman need return from the hunt without a few horns, if he cares for trophies of that kind; for the buffalo is distributed practically all over Africa, from South Africa up to the desolate tracts of the Sahara, from the sea in the west to the sea in the east, and lives both on the plains and high up in the mountains. And while a herd of buffaloes a thousand strong is certainly not seen every day, it is far from being a curiosity. There are quite a number of varieties, from the massive Kaffir buffalo of the east coast, via the smaller Sudan type, to the dwarf forms of the Ituri forest; and they are of every shade between black and red, from the ebony-black Kaffir buffalo to the light-red dwarf buffalo.

One sometimes hears hunters who are more or less casual visitors to Africa speak of buffalo-hunting with a deprecatory shrug of the shoulders. Lion and elephant are what they want. Let me assure the reader that nothing could be more wrong than this contemptuous attitude towards buffalo-hunting. It is good and dangerous sport and, properly conducted, demands conspicuous sporting qualities.

The buffalo is one of the most dangerous beasts in Africa; he attacks swiftly and unexpectedly and with a strength that is almost elemental. He has a perfect genius for utilizing the advantages which a difficult country can give, so that one often does not discover him till the last moment. When in good fettle he never attacks simply from malice or pleasure in killing, but only when he thinks that attack is his only way of escape; but if he is in a bad humor — his temper is irritable and undependable — he may attack without the least provocation. Ill humor may be due to the fact that the animal has an old wound which irritates him, or that he has some internal complaint. One never knows where one is with a buffalo, and therefore one must always be on one's guard when after him. But he is dangerous in yet another way. Of all African animals the buffalo is the only one which has a hereditary instinct, when wounded and pursued, to leave his tracks, lie in ambush, and attack from the flank. Many an unsuspecting hunter has lost his life through this maneuver.

In this connection, I may as well rectify a common misapprehension. The buffalo does not charge with his head lowered. All the pictures which show him with his head down at the decisive moment are inaccurate. The blazing eyes are right enough, but he charges with head outstretched. Only in the very last second does the buffalo lower his horns and deliver his blow. When the victim has fallen to the ground, he lies down upon him and crushes the body to pulp with one shoulder.

Buffalo meat tastes good and can be prepared in many different ways. The blacks are fond of it dried.

In old days a buffalo hide was worth about £12 and was a valued article of merchandise among the blacks, who made their shields of the leather. But since the British Government has prohibited the carrying of shields the hides have had no great market value. The prohibition is one of the measures taken by the English to discourage a warlike spirit among the black tribes.

I myself have had many adventures with buffaloes which confirm what I have just said of their habits and characteristics. Once I was out walking in the country with a friend, and as we did not mean to shoot we had left our gun-bearers a long way behind. Suddenly the quiet was broken by the angry bellowing of a buffalo. In contrast to human beings, an animal never attacks without first announcing its intention; and the bellowing meant that we had better look out for ourselves. The next second the buffalo burst out of the brushwood and made straight for me with head outstretched. There was nothing for it but to take to my heels.

BUFFALOES

I tore downhill as hard as I could go, but it was not many seconds before I found that the buffalo was faster than I. Although I was unarmed the situation was not so desperate this time, however — there were plenty of trees among which to maneuver. I flung my arms round the nearest trunk and spun round it.

The buffalo put on the brake a little too quickly, and the hill was steep; he swung round and sat down on his haunches. I wondered if the game was to continue. But the buffalo had clearly no further inclination. He suddenly gave up and proceeded down the slope at a much more sober pace. That was his misfortune. Before he had got out of range my gun-bearer had reached the tree, and bang! an instantaneous and painless death. When we examined the beast later we found that I had almost performed an act of charity; the body was emaciated and riddled with old shot wounds, and it was without doubt the animal's sufferings that had caused the bitterness and ill humor which were the fundamental reasons for his attack on me.

A similar incident happened soon afterwards when I was out for a ramble in the country with my wife, though that time, luckily, I had my rifle under my arm. On one side of us the plain lay empty, on the other was wood. We were walking along the outskirts of the wood. Suddenly there was a crashing noise among the trees, a short bellow, and the buffalo was right on us. No one who has not had a similar experience can imagine with what extraordinary swiftness the attack is made.

I had to shoot from the hip — I had no chance of raising the rifle to my shoulder. The distance was not six yards, and the huge beast fell in the very instant of attack. Where was he hit? We examined the body thoroughly, but could find no bullet-hole. The whole thing seemed a bit of a mystery, but when the body was cut up, the riddle was solved; the bullet had gone in at the mouth, knocked out two teeth, and lodged in the neck — a fresh proof that the buffalo charges with head outstretched. This rascal, too, had a few old wounds from encounters with men and beasts, which had embittered his life and finally led to his desperate resolve to take vengeance.

I have already indicated that the buffalo is in a marked degree a thinking animal. He is most loyal to the family tie, and times without number I have witnessed instances of his sense of duty towards his mate and young.

The film company Svensk Filmindustri was in Africa a few years ago, and I gave the expedition a little help with its close-up photographs of big game. One day we were photographing buffaloes. Our job was to get the buffaloes to come to the camera, instead of the reverse. A corps of well-trained boys, under my orders, had been long and hard at work on a herd of several hundred buffaloes, trying to make them approach the well-concealed camera. All those fine bulls with their splendid horns were regular film stars, so we spared no effort.

But things would not go right. They had taken up their position in a copse of small trees, whence, with necks outstretched and ears pricked up, they kept a hostile eye on our proceedings without moving an inch in the direction we wished. We waved our blankets and fired shots to frighten them. In vain! Not one of them would be frightened, and we stood there looking pretty silly, I must admit.

I simply could not understand it. Under normal conditions our operation ought to have succeeded long before — something unusual was in the wind. I had recourse to my glass and began to examine the countryside. Aha! There lay the key to the riddle. Behind the copse was a valley, and there I detected the cow buffaloes with their calves, quietly stealing away to a place of safety on the other side of the crest, while the bulls covered and secured their retreat in the manner I have just described. Their task was to keep us in check, and they did so. And when the last calf had disappeared below the horizon, the bulls began their strategic retreat in perfect order, and the photographers got nothing that time.

I remember another incident on the same expedition which proves just as strikingly, if not more so, that the buffalo can be more astute than a general staff. A gang of natives had been ordered to act as beaters and try to drive a herd of buffaloes towards the camera. Things looked promising at first. The herd had moved in the desired direction, but suddenly the higher command decided that the pursuers were becoming too bold. About twenty buffaloes were detached from the main body and delivered a lightning attack on the beaters, who naturally took to their heels. When the pressure from that quarter had been relieved the patrol rejoined the main body, which executed a skillful flank movement and avoided the (from their standpoint) undesired contact with the cameraman.

One day at my farm a Negro came and reported that a bull buffalo, which I had been trying to shoot for a long time, had taken refuge in a thick copse near by. With some friends who happened to

BUFFALOES

be visiting me I went to the copse at once in order, as a beginning, to get the fellow to come out. The job was neither easy nor safe, but I had five faithful black hunters to help me, with ample experience of the buffalo's habits and caprices. They went into the brushwood and began beating, while the white men held the passes through which the buffalo might be expected to come out. Time passed. Now and again we heard the beaters' shouts, cries, and hand-clappings. Suddenly a cry for help was heard from inside the copse, and one of my black friends came running up and reported that the bull had attacked one of their number and severely injured him. I plunged into the brushwood and found the poor devil badly hurt, but despite his serious injuries he insisted on being present when the criminal was tracked down and punished, as he now must be without delay.

"You mustn't go without me," the wounded man cried, clinging fast to my legs.

But I had to do so, and a few hours later I shot the buffalo. The war-dance round the dead beast was danced with an enthusiasm which can be more easily imagined than described.

I have often followed herds over the countryside for days and weeks on end and seen the buffalo living his life undisturbed and ignorant of the presence of mankind.

He begins his day at four in the morning, rises heavily from his couch and begins to graze. He takes a mouthful here, a mouthful there, snatching the grass from the dew-drenched tufts; the herd is continually in movement. The bullocks meet in playful conflict with lowered heads; the cows jostle each other, lowing. On the edge of the herd the huge leader is pursuing one of his lady-loves; he is quite capable of keeping the younger gentlemen at a distance. Now and then a cow turns anxiously to look for her calf, which is gamboling cheerfully about at a rash distance from its mother.

The herd moves all the time; it drinks, then grazes again. At eight the sun is hot. The beasts, lazy and half asleep, move under shady mimosa trees or lie down in the long screening grass to chew the cud.

And when the sun, on his journey across the heavens, sinks towards the west, the buffaloes become active again. Once more they graze, once more they drink, once more the herd moves restlessly about. When darkness comes on they look for a resting-place for the night, almost always a new one and as well protected as possible against the buffalo's worst enemies — men and lions!

BUFFALOES

But before I leave my friend the buffalo I must say something about Lottie. I was out buffalo-hunting for a museum and had shot two fine specimens in the morning. In the afternoon I got two more, and it was then that I met Lottie. She was an exhausted little calf, left behind by the herd, and my boy Juma caught her with ease. Juma had to hurry off to the nearest Negro village to get milk, and after that meal the calf Lottie and I became the best friends in the world.

But it was not long before the buffalo showed her aggressive instincts. If Lottie suspected that I was in the slightest danger, she would attack to defend me. We were together day and night. When night came and I went to bed, she always lay down in such a position that she touched me, so that she should know immediately if I meant to leave her. Lottie was more vigilant and defiant than a watchdog; she guarded my tent with all the buffalo's meditative obstinacy. At the slightest noise from outside she rose, ready to defend her newly acquired friend.

Lottie grew up into a large buffalo. Her shoulders and chest were terrifying, but her eyes were mild. Our friendship lasted till Lottie died — of some internal complaint, presumably rinderpest. I mourned for her sincerely, and still do so today.

IV. *Elephants*

It was up in the Belgian Congo — to be more exact, in the neighborhood of Avakubi, whither chance had taken me. For want of better occupation I turned to elephant-hunting, and for company I had a party of highly respectable cannibals, who had for the moment abandoned the hereditary bill of fare. I could hardly have found better trackers; intimately acquainted with the elephant's mentality and habits, they had an instinct which sometimes seemed magical.

One day I had wounded a big bull, which took to flight along an elephant track. He went off at a tremendous pace with the trackers close at his heels — and the lads who followed in his wake were confident of victory. For they knew that they had set a spear trap a little farther along the track, which the elephant could not escape. He was rushing straight to disaster; his doom was sealed.

"The falling spear" is an old tradition in Africa. Generation after generation of blacks have killed elephants in this way — once the animal has been got on the right track, the trap has been considered infallible. The mechanism is simple. A spear has a weight attached to it and is set up in a tree-top right over the elephant track; a very fine thread is stretched across the track, and when the elephant rushes by and breaks the thread the spear falls. The natives have estimated the elephant's speed and the distance between the trees with the skill of a professor of mathematics and have fixed the spear at such a height that when it falls it will enter the elephant's body at a vital point.

My black comrades' expectancy and excitement on the occasion I am describing was, therefore, quite natural. But scarcely five yards from the point at which the thread was drawn the elephant suddenly turned aside and returned to the track when he had passed the danger-point. He knew exactly where he was in peril.

While speaking of this trap, I may mention that

the natives have exploited for practical purposes the elephant's instinctive fear of the fine threads which have sent so many of his ancestors to happier hunting-grounds. To protect their banana plantations in the forest against visits from elephants, the natives stretch a fine liana creeper between the trees, and that creeper is a more effective protection against destructive animals than a wooden stockade — as I can testify from my own experience. The suspicious elephant scents danger — he loves bananas, but will not risk his life for a square meal.

When I came to Africa it was not long before my ideas of the elephant, his nature and mentality, were thoroughly revised. Like most other people, I thought him a mild, good-natured animal. And what is he like in reality? When you are out shooting one day and suddenly find yourself the hunted instead of the hunter, with death trumpeting furiously hard at your heels, it is no use appealing to the elephant's mildness and good nature. There are other adjectives which describe him better — savage and vindictive. I spoke just now of his instinct. The right word is sense — sense and reasoning power.

His sight is not so good. His little pig's eyes are of small assistance to his powers of observation; his hearing, on the contrary, is sharp, thanks to his enormous ears. He can hear the slightest sound at a great distance and judge exactly from where it comes. Trunk in air, he can scent what is a mile away better than a dog. When I have disturbed an elephant he has always gone down wind. But when he is looking for a lair for the night he goes up wind — rightly judging that in doing so he has a great advantage in his fine sense of smell, which tells him at great distances what he ought to do or not do. Like the buffalo, he reflects and draws conclusions, which very seldom play him false.

Of all forms of hunting, elephant-hunting is the most trying to the sportsman. The elephant covers about three yards with every step and forces his way through jungle and thick undergrowth which defy man. And, unlike other animals, the elephant can be completely independent of waterholes; he can go without water, if need be, for many days on end.

You need not be a coward for your hair to stand on end with fear when you are charged by an elephant. You suddenly become so fearfully small. There is a thing called sportsman's nerves which is responsible for many misses — and there is ample excuse for an unsteady hand. A mistake of a fraction of a second, the smallest error of judgment in distance or hit, may be as good as a death sentence, and heaven help the man who has not a clear brain at the decisive moment. Unless the bullet from your large-caliber gun hits heart or brain you may as well send your remembrances to those at home; so he who goes elephant-hunting had better take a few thorough lessons beforehand in the creature's anatomy.

I indicated above that the native trackers have an astonishing flair for the elephant's habits and tracks. But they are just as closely watched by the elephant, and it is a question whether he does not know more about them than they do about him. One day I was following the spoor of four bull elephants in the heart of the Ituri forest — spoor of the previous day, left towards the evening. It led me to some native huts. But what a sight! The most hideous devastation. The banana plantation was wrecked as though by a cyclone; not a single tree was left standing. What the elephants had not devoured they had pulled up. It was as bad with the fig trees, from whose bark the people make clothes; they were completely destroyed, and the durra fields had been trampled down and rendered worthless. One of the huts, used for the storage of seed, had also been pulled down; the whole place, in fact, the result of many years' work, had been totally ruined.

ELEPHANTS

As I stood there contemplating the disaster, the sorely afflicted family came back, and the poor people's feelings can easily be imagined. A public duty had compelled them to go away for two days — they had been to pay their taxes to the British Government's collector — and that journey had cost them all they possessed.

"Everything is destroyed," said one of the men sadly. "It is the first time we have left our home unguarded for two years, and see what has happened."

"Shoot the elephants for us," another cried.

Quite right — the crime must be punished. That was only logical and fair. I put myself at the head of the punitive expedition, got on the criminals' tracks, and came up with them about four in the afternoon. They proved to have poor tusks — under ordinary circumstances I should not have thought of shooting any of them — but now justice had to be done. I sent a bullet through the heart of the biggest and let the ruined family have the meat, the sale of which must have brought in three or four shillings — a minor salve to the wound.

A luxuriant and variegated growth of legends has sprung up concerning the elephant's life and habits. It is asserted, *inter alia*, that one need not be tender-hearted to be moved to tears by his helpfulness towards wounded comrades, and one incident after another is quoted in proof of this. After nearly twenty-five years spent among African elephants I can affirm that I have never seen an instance of this helpfulness, though I once thought that a scene acted under my eyes might be regarded as lending support to the assertion.

It happened like this. When shooting near the Nile, I was once unlucky enough to wound an elephant, which fled across a watercourse — one of the Nile's most insignificant tributaries. I followed, of course, but got no farther than the bank of the stream. Here a canoe had to be procured, and while some of my boys were trying to get one, I was able to follow my wounded elephant's proceedings from the bank through my glasses. A *coup de grâce* was out of the question; the distance was too great.

On the other side of the river lay a plain, and farther away the forest began; I guessed that my elephant would seek shelter there. But he could not get so far; he sank to his knees, exhausted by loss of blood, and at that moment another elephant with very large tusks appeared on the scene. First the newcomer went slowly round his wounded comrade — a meditative inspection — and immediately afterwards gave him a push from behind so that he rose to his feet again.

"Oho!" I thought, not a little surprised, and hoped to see how the elephant would help his friend to escape.

But the thought was hardly framed in my mind when the good Samaritan, with a deafening trumpeting, made a flank attack on the wounded beast, so that he tumbled down again; after which the benefactor, still trumpeting, trotted off and disappeared in the forest. At that moment my boys arrived with the canoe, and a few minutes later I was able to administer the *coup de grâce* to the fallen giant.

Then I was able to observe the traces left by the good Samaritan's work of charity — and they were no trifle. The friendly shove from behind had left ugly scars, and the wounds in the flank were so large and deep that I could put both my hands into them. My final shot, of course, put a quicker end to the animal's sufferings, but otherwise it is fairly certain that he could not have survived the treatment he had received from the other elephant.

What can have caused the second elephant to behave as he did? Just what makes a dog bite his best friend when the latter is beaten. Was it a desire to free his wounded comrade from his sufferings? I think the question must be left open; at any rate, his conduct was dictated by no urge to relieve the other beast or to help him — of that I am sure.

But the ghost elephant in the Belgian Congo was no legend. The first I heard of him was from a friend of mine while I was making preparations for a safari in those regions.

"It's right in your line," he said. "He's a super-elephant, and he's no myth either, for I've seen him myself. The people have christened him Jaho — which means unconquerable — and he is unconquerable, with such long tusks that they make marks on the ground as he goes along."

Hum! Long tusks are heavy tusks — and one can get ten shillings a pound for ivory, as I mentioned earlier. It was not avarice, however, that drove me to the regions inhabited by Jaho, but the urge to shoot a ghostly elephant which must be in league with the powers of darkness, to judge from all the circumstantial stories of his ability to appear and disappear in the most mysterious way.

And when I reached the place, my enthusiasm was not cooled, but the reverse. Jaho's name was on the lips of every black; he was regarded as a supernatural being. No spear could kill him, no poison acted on him, and the man was not born of woman who was cunning enough to lure Jaho into a pit trap. For a whole month I lived the life of a native among the blacks, and every day I followed the ghost elephant's spoor without result. I saw where he had been and what he had been doing, but of himself I saw not so much as the tip of his tail. Till one night . . .

I was awakened an hour before dawn by the natives shouting that an elephant had begun to break the banana trees in their plantation. I got on my legs with some difficulty, but became wide awake all of a sudden on discovering that my clothes had gone. But it was not only my clothes; my sun-helmet had gone too, and, worst of all, my gun and its case. A thief had been at work during the night and pinched all my belongings. But no Sherlock Holmes was needed; the light-fingered fellow could be no other than one of my black boys, Marobe by name; and as soon as I had managed to organize a search party and sent it out to look for the thief, I went off after the ghost elephant — a hunter with no gun, a blanket over his shoulders, and a pillow as a sun-helmet.

Meanwhile Jaho had eaten his fill of my hosts' bananas. I found him soon after sunrise in a swamp, rounding off his morning meal with a little grass. Rumor had not lied; he was an unusually fine beast, with tusks the like of which I had never seen. He paid no attention to me, but simply ignored my existence. I sat for four hours wearing my blanket and pillow — I think I must have presented a rather curious appearance — and watched him finish his meal with dignity, quench his thirst with the tepid water of the swamp, and having concluded the lengthy procedure which is known as " the elephant's morning toilet," slowly withdraw. That was the last I saw of him.

When I got back to the hut I had ample time to ponder over the loss of my belongings. What I could not understand at first was how Marobe had been able to lay hands on my gun-case, which for safety's sake I always used as a pillow. A brown stain on the mosquito net afforded the solution to the problem; the thieving scoundrel had blown opium smoke under the net, which had made my sleep so heavy that he had been able to carry out his evil plans undisturbed. The inhaling of opium explained, too, why my head had felt so heavy and my legs so stiff when I had been awakened.

It was not so strange that Marobe should have been specially anxious to get at my gun-case; he had seen that I used it as a cash-box, and of course it was the money he wanted. But here his plan miscarried. I had taken five thousand francs out of my " bank " the day before and sent it to the town to pay for a new elephant license, and after that not more than a hundred francs were left. I felt that, in any case, Marobe would have little joy of the money, for the cook, who was in command of the search party, was a good tracker, and it was proved a few hours later that my instinct had been quite right. The arrival of the party was dramatic; Marobe was led in on a rope, with a noose round his neck, and his hands tied behind his back. The cook told me that they had given him a good thrashing as soon as they caught him, just to start with, and my servants, to show their disgust at his action, began alternately to spit in his face and hit him on the mouth — a torture which I naturally stopped at once. At the same time I could not let the escapade go unpunished, but next day sent the misguided youth to the police in charge of the cook, with a letter describing what had happened.

But that is not quite the end of the story of the ghost elephant. About six months later I met a friend, a Dutchman by nationality, in a bar in London, and told him about Jaho. He listened with shining eyes.

"I'll shoot that elephant," he declared. Nor was it a vain boast; he did. When he came out to Africa some time afterwards, we searched for Jaho together, and after only a week's hunting my friend brought him down. The tusks weighed 285 lb. and fetched alone more than £250. Even ghost elephants can have bad luck.

Early one inclement morning I found a promising spoor not far from my camp in the Congo forest. The impressions of the feet in the soil were as large as an ordinary hip-bath, and although my guide informed me that he knew the elephant in question well and that it had no tusks at all, I determined to pursue the hunt and see for myself.

We followed the spoor for an hour at a brisk pace. Suddenly we heard him; the crashing of a broken tree told us that he had not yet finished his breakfast. I left the blacks behind and crept forward alone. Not a sound was heard — perhaps he had made off. Then I heard a faint crackling behind the tree against which I was leaning. I looked cautiously over my shoulder. Yes, there was the tip of his trunk swinging only a few yards from my feet. What about his tusks? I ran my eyes up his trunk inch by inch, but no tusks could I see.

I began to retreat noiselessly. The least breath of wind or a broken twig might cost me my life. When I was twenty steps away he got wind of me. About turn and off! Then he stopped, waved his trunk, and when he again got wind of me and the blacks, who had now come up, he uttered a shrill trumpeting and came for us. We all rushed away, but as he came crashing on much faster than we could run, I jumped aside and stopped. The elephant halted again in a little clearing in the forest and snuffed. Then he stood motionless for some minutes only ten steps away from me, with outstretched ears, listening intently. But all was quiet, and, sure that he had scared us away, he ambled off.

I lowered my elephant-gun; my pulse became normal again; the boys came up and the guide pointed out, with a broad grin, that he had been right.

"*Pembe ata kidogo, bwana!* (Not a sign of tusks, master!)"

Another spoor — smaller and not so fresh. But perhaps it might lead us to others. I followed it all day, and not till sunset did I come upon an elephant with hundred-pound tusks. A bullet in the ear-hole ended his life.

A few days later, in the same district, I found two fresh night spoors. A little later a third joined them, and they went together into very high elephant grass. The beasts got wind of me at fifty yards and rushed off, but soon stopped again. Then they stood motionless for at least half an hour, and I had no choice but to creep up to them alone. I knew that one of them was standing rather to the left of the two others, and stole up to him, noiselessly, inch by inch. This took a quarter of an hour. Only those who have been through it know what a strain, how exhausting to the nerves, such a quarter of an hour can be.

I saw him from ten paces off — no tusks. I crept noiselessly away. All went well. Then I went after the others. They got wind of me and rushed away, one to the right and one straight ahead. I waited for my gun-bearer and went after the last-named beast. Soon we saw him again, standing still and listening. I knew he would charge if he heard us, and as we were in fairly open undergrowth I raised my gun to my shoulder, aimed at the ear-hole, and fired.

But either he was not standing at the angle I judged or the shot had not hit him at the point intended — at any rate he did not fall, but took a step forward and stopped again to listen.

"Shoot!" my gun-bearer whispered.

The elephant heard and charged. The bullet from the other barrel did not stop him. I had been leaning against a small tree; I jumped sideways, but fell and lay stretched on the ground with the heavy gun in my right hand. I could not have moved even if I had wished to do so.

ELEPHANTS

The elephant detected my scent on the bark of the tree and flung the tree to the ground; he fell on his knees and drove his tusks into the earth down to the roots, one on each side of the trunk; got up again and gave me — thinking me dead — a menacing look from his little pig's eyes, and went crashing and thundering away through the jungle. Not till I had whistled and shouted for a long time did my boys arrive, and when they saw me unhurt, astonishment was perhaps more clearly depicted on their faces than joy.

The same afternoon I came upon two more elephants. They were standing in a large wood, about a hundred yards apart. I had two boys with me and left them a short distance behind. I fired at ten paces, but with the same result as in the morning. The elephant took just one step forward and halted to listen. Then one of the boys lost his head and began to run, the elephant after him with deafening trumpetings. As he rushed past me, I fired when I caught a glimpse of him through a gap in the brushwood. Then he rushed after the other boy, who bolted in his turn. More crashing and trumpeting. Then all was quiet. Only a broken branch in the distance told me that he had gone on his way.

That was not a day I wish to see repeated; but I

shall always remember, with mingled astonishment and terror, that elephant kneeling at my feet.

I once went out hunting in Uganda with a license for twenty-five elephants. After three hours' tracking I caught sight of three elephants, but only their backs were visible in the long grass. For a moment I had the idea that I might perhaps get a chance of a shot if I climbed up on my gun-bearer's shoulders, but at that moment I caught sight of an ant-heap near by, raising its conical head above the desert of grass. I ordered my gun-bearer to stay at the foot of the stack, forbade him to fire, and clambered up.

Thank goodness! This view was not so bad. But the summit of the heap was hardly bigger than the top of a sailor's cap, so that there was no room for any antics. The three elephants moved slowly towards the stack with the wind behind them, which explained their not detecting me. I chose a bull with large tusks, raised the heavy elephant-gun, and fired.

Bang!

I had counted on the elephant falling, but not on my keeping him company. The recoil made me overbalance; I slithered helplessly down from the top of the stack and measured my length on the

FOUR ELEPHANTS SHOT ON A SIX DAYS' HUNT
The tusks average 115 lb.

HERD OF ELEPHANTS EMERGING FROM A SWAMP

ground beneath. The two remaining elephants now rushed towards the stack and in a moment were standing quite close to me, trunks in the air. I rose inch by inch. I fired at the nearest animal right between the eyes. He collapsed only a few steps away, and as the other turned at the same moment, I shot him in the shoulder.

Then I beckoned to my boy and we went off home, shaken by the excitement such a moment affords. Poor lad — he was caught and killed by an infuriated elephant five years ago.

I am not ashamed to say that I was frightened myself. The man who declares that he is not afraid of elephants is either an ignoramus or a liar.

Another trio of elephants caused me more amusement than alarm. I had been pursuing three elephants for a long time in a dense forest without being able to catch sight of them for long enough to decide whether their tusks justified a shot. My only hope was that they would at last come out into more open country, and they did so late in the afternoon, after a nerve-racking chase. In the midst of the primeval forest they found a glade, perhaps a few acres in extent, pale-green in the evening sun and charming to the eye. The giants looked round, spread out their big sail-like ears, and trumpeted loudly several times. Then they began to move solemnly to and fro, with tails up and trunks in air. I thought they had got wind of me.

Then one of the beasts suddenly went up to one of the others, laid his trunk on his forehead, and set his tusks against the other's. Then began a wrestling match which made the earth shake. Both combatants faltered and took new grip. Ivories clinked, muscles quivered, the beasts' huge strength was strained to the uttermost. Then one of them fell at full length on his side, while the victor delivered a deafening fanfare.

Number three, who during the conflict had displayed his enthusiasm by waving his head, flinging huge sods of grass up in the air and rushing to and fro, now approached the conqueror. They met forehead to forehead; all their strength was exerted. Not a sound was heard, but their bodies quivered with the exertion; their feet slipped away when they took purchase; every nerve was at full strain. The whole surroundings seemed to be charged with a strong nervous tension while the two giants measured their colossal strength. I wonder if even the birds were not silent.

Then one of the champions fell on his haunches, and the fresh triumph was greeted with a fanfare. But at the same moment there came a gust of wind, this time from the wrong quarter, and when the elephants saw that a human being had been watching their play, they rushed panic-stricken into the jungle.

I stood there alone with a sight I shall never forget struck into my memory.

How does the elephant spend his day when unmolested by that tiresome individual called man? The answer to that question is short and easy — in satisfying a gluttonous appetite. The elephant eats a colossal, an incredible amount. At the same time he is a gourmet rather than a gourmand and will readily take the trouble to go a long way, miles and miles, if there is some attractive delicacy at his journey's end. The human gourmet knows when crab tastes best and when salmon is most delicious. The elephant's dainties hang from the trees, and he knows just as well at what times of the year his suppliers offer the best quality of goods — when the banyan tree is bearing and when the fan palm's exquisite fruit is ripe. He wanders enormous distances along the elephant tracks, trodden for thousands and thousands of years, to satisfy his craving for delicacies; he knows that the leaves of every bush taste different at different times of the year — according as they are full of sap or the heat makes the vegetation less juicy — and adapts himself to the circumstances.

The elephant rises with the sun. His clamorous stomach has been crying out for food for some time — and he does not let it cry in vain. He does his morning toilet while he grazes, and, like the buffalo, he covers considerable distances while feeding. Not till towards midday, when the rays of the sun become too fierce, does he seek out some shady tree and take his siesta under it, as a rule standing, though it does occasionally happen that he lies down. But at four or five he resumes his itinerant search for provender, which only night can interrupt.

He loves water and subscribes readily to the doctrine that bathing makes for health. As I mentioned above, he can go without drinking water for several days on end, if need be. But during the rainy season he revels in the water, and when he is not rolling in it he uses his trunk to apply douches to his massive carcass. When the dry season deprives him of this pleasure he sprinkles his back with sand and earth instead — perhaps it may cool him to some extent. In any case the layer of earth protects him against insect bites, when the birds, especially the white herons, which usually help to keep insects away, are lazy or holiday-making.

ELEPHANTS

At the water-holes where the elephant quenches his thirst, he has his own special tactics. The knowledge that it is dangerous to drink by moonlight is hereditary in his blood; for many hundreds of generations the natives have bombarded him with poisoned arrows from the tree-tops round the water as soon as the moon has emerged from the clouds. He therefore, as a rule, takes good care to avoid this danger; he drinks quickly and does not stop afterwards till he has placed a mile or two between himself and the water-hole.

He is fond of resting for the night at the foot of an ant-heap — such pillows are plentiful in Africa. His sleep is heavy and anything but noiseless; there is a saying " to snore like a hippopotamus," but the elephant is a good second.

For some reason or other, fears of the total extinction of the elephant are sometimes expressed. Allow me to declare that there is no danger! If anything, the opposite is the case. I cannot give any exact figures without reference to the elephant statistics, but there is no doubt that the race is increasing. Drastic intervention by the State will most likely he demanded, to protect the natives' property and keep the elephant within bounds. Even today herds a thousand strong are no rarity.

The elephant is pretty equally distributed over almost the whole of Africa; when it is said that the traveler can go the whole way across the continent, from the east to the west coast, along elephant tracks, it is no exaggeration. In the tropical heat of the coast, in the Galla desert's ocean of scrub, in the cedar and bamboo woods of the mountains, which the night frost covers with a white shroud each morning, and in the papyrus swamps of the Nile — everywhere the elephant is at home. He wanders in the gloom of the Ituri forest, through the endless marshes of the Congo River, up towards the sandy Sahara desert, and right to the fever-stricken regions on the west coast.

In the Haut-Uele district of the Belgian Congo near the Sudan frontier, the blacks were always talking about elephants with four tusks. They had a special name for them and attributed to them every possible supernatural quality. Elephants with four tusks are the leaders of the herds and are always protected by the other animals, which, the natives say, explains the fact that they are so rarely seen.

My friend the black chief Wando, of whom I shall speak again later, told me a great deal about them and said he knew of the existence of such

ELEPHANTS

commanders-in-chief in several places. My then gun-bearer, Mafutamingi, confirmed this and assured me that he had three times met elephants with four tusks. I asked Wando if he could not secure me a specimen — either direct me to the places where he knew they were or send out one of his elephant-hunters to shoot one. He did both. For more than a month I hunted four-tuskers in the regions Wando indicated, with his boys, and inspected hundreds of elephants, but they were all of the two-tusk kind. But the hunter I had sent out had better luck and was actually able to display the head of an elephant with three tusks. The left tusk had been formed double, but the root was in the same socket — the best comparison is with a philopena almond.

Since I hunted there, a number of elephants with four tusks and more have been shot, so there is no doubt they exist in many places. The four tusks are, of course, a malformation which is unlikely to be hereditary. Tuskless elephants, on the other hand, occur all over Africa, but in no place where I have hunted were they so numerous as in the Belgian Congo. It is possible that tusklessness is hereditary, and if so a watchful Game Department ought to see that such beasts are shot. Curiously enough, no white elephant has ever been encountered in Africa.

Lastly, not to be unfair to Hans, I must say a few words about him too, as Lottie has received her own special mention in an earlier chapter. One day when out elephant-hunting in long grass, I heard a shrill trumpeting. My black trackers explored the ground closely from the tops of some high trees, but could see no sign of an elephant. Most mysterious! Was it a new ghost elephant? We looked at each other in surprise and interrogation.

" I heard him quite clearly over there," said my gun-bearer, pointing.

" So did I," " So did I," the others assured me unanimously; there was only some little difference of opinion as to the direction in which the trumpetings had been heard. Suddenly they were heard again, and it was not many minutes before we discovered the animal — a dear little baby elephant which had fallen into a deep pit and could not get out again. But the little fellow could send out his SOS signals; he was not so very little, for that matter, despite his tender age. I should say he was about a year old.

We waited in perfect silence for an hour or two, thinking that the mother would come to look for her child, but fear was stronger than mother-love. As it was clear that mamma had left baby to his fate, I had no choice but to adopt him myself. We shoveled earth into the pit, the young elephant himself trampled it into the ground, and in this way we soon got him out. After a few hours of caresses, friendly talk, and feeding with juicy grass, we became good friends. The very next day he followed me like a dog, and at night he lay on the floor by my bed. As time passed he came to take up a good deal of room in the house, and it was rather inconvenient at times, but what will one not put up with for one's friends?

About six months later I had to go away, and as there could be no question of taking Hans with me on the long journey, I had to leave him in charge of my servants. I do not doubt for a moment that they looked after Hans to the best of their ability, but either he was no longer happy, or perhaps it was a longing for the wide open spaces that drove him away again. Anyhow, when I came back he had disappeared, and perhaps it was just as well.

V. *Lions*

OF all the faithful animals I have had during my pretty varied life, there is none that can in any way be compared with Kom. It was somewhere about the spring of 1925 when a native appeared with him and laid him in my arms — the sweetest little creature in the world, soft and pleasant to hold, with four feeble little pegs which could hardly bear him across the floor — a little lion prince, only a few days old. The Negro had found him behind a bush out in the country and had run home for dear life with him, desperately afraid lest the royal mother should come after him and give him a nip from behind.

"I thought the cub would be happy with you, *bwana*," he said simply.

And I venture to say that he was. I lavished as much tenderness and care on him as it was in my power to do — in the dependent position in which, for my sins, I then was. Untoward events had compelled me to sign a labor contract as carter at a saw-mill; from early morning to late evening I was out in the wood with my team of oxen, but Kom was always with me. He was quite independent at the age of six weeks, and his intelligence was more developed than that of a puppy of the same age. And how he could play! There was no limit to his powers of invention in thinking of mischievous pranks. Funniest of all was when he came into illegal possession of newspapers and books. In two swift seconds they were transformed into grotesque lumps of paper with which he played ball to his heart's delight — until the unpleasant hour of discovery struck, for there was something else which struck, and that he did not like.

Punishment is an inevitable part of every affectionate upbringing, and naturally Kom experienced it. It was not pleasant; but it had to be. He knew exactly what was allowed and what was not, but temptation was too strong for him when he caught sight of a bundle of newspapers, which made such a nice crackling noise when he tore it into a thousand pieces with his sharp claws. Temperamental like all cats, he could not bear punishment; he crept into a corner, wept like a child for long after, and would have nothing to do with his master — firmly determined to heap coals of fire upon his head. On such occasions it was best to take no notice of him — if I had shown the least sign of regret at having punished him he would have got the upper hand of me. If, on the contrary, I left him alone and let him have his cry out he never bore malice — incredibly sociable creature as he was — and when happy relations were restored between us he was beside himself with joy.

At six months Kom was a fine big lion, but not once during those first six months had the real lion's claws emerged from his pads. He went about among the oxen as a good friend, and they were no more afraid of him than of a fly — they did not even notice his leonine smell. But on one occasion the instinct of a wild beast flared up in Kom. I had been obliged to shoot an ox which had broken its leg, and Kom was present at the execution. The instant the ox fell and the smell of blood came to Kom's nostrils, he was upon the fallen animal with one stately bound and a kingly roar; he began to lap its blood, and it was not advisable for any of the blacks to try to approach him. He defended his booty till he had eaten his fill, and when it was over he slipped back into civilized life as if nothing had happened.

Kom was perfectly at home among the belts and saws in the mill, and the black workmen took no more notice of him than if he had been a gentle big dog. He seemed positively to enjoy himself among the hissing, screaming machinery. But he did not like the sirens. One morning he happened to be between two of them when they blew simultaneously to summon the men to work. Little Kom was terrified. He set off, a good deal faster than the Mombasa-Nairobi train, for the place where he always sought shelter when danger threatened — my bed. My bed was his sanctuary; he slept in it at night and crept under it by day when he felt his security in any way endangered.

Kom loved a ride in a car, and used to stand inside with his paws on the front seat. Once he tried jumping out when the car was at full speed, but he did not try it again. He had caught sight of a fat hen, and the temptation was too strong — at her! But was he killed? Not a bit of it. He crawled up out of a huge cloud of dust, a bit dazed, with his tail between his legs and no hen. If ever anyone was glad to get into a car it was Kom on that occasion.

We remained together for many months after this, but when my contract came to an end we had to part. I puzzled my head as to what I was to do with my friend Kom. I could not, unhappily, take him with me, and it would have been cruel to shut him up in a cage. To hand him over to the blacks was out of the question; they could not manage Kom. Should I restore him to the freedom he had never lost — in other words, let him return to the steppe? That too would have been a merciless act, for a cruel fate would have met him there. The only way out was to let him end his days in a painless manner — and this was done.

Kom taught me a great deal in his short life. All that I know of the lion's mentality I got from him; and it was of inestimable value to me later. I came to know the lion's capricious temper, which can change from good to ill humor like thunder and sunshine; I learned his language and found out whether it was rage, hunger, or love that sounded in his voice; and it is a consoling thought to me that all his days were happy and carefree.

If I were to give a detailed account of all the lions I have shot or fired at, I fear that I should be too long-winded. I will content myself with relating some episodes which throw more or less light on the lion's mentality and his reactions in certain situations.

My earliest meeting with a lion was during my very first expedition in Africa, when I was out collecting workers for my coffee plantation. We had pitched camp near a water-hole — a quiet, peaceful place it seemed, but nevertheless the night was a trifle disturbed. The tropical night symphony was in too full blast. The crickets chirped more furiously than usual — it sounds like a thousand bows at work behind the bridge of a violin; the jackals howled far off, and at times the air resounded with the beating of heavy wings. Suddenly there was a moment's silence. The invisible conductor had silenced the music for a fraction of a second to make the famous solo singer's interjection the more effective. There came the long-drawn, melodious roar of a lion, ending in a staccato " huh-uh-uh."

I listened to the sound with every nerve drawn tight, as when I used to lie in bed at Näsbyholm and listen to the thunder; and I wondered, just as I had done then: would the sound come nearer? Another rumbling sound, duller, angrier than the first, but at the same distance from the tent. What was the royal route tonight? There — for a third time! Right by the tent, if you please! Were we to receive a nocturnal visitor?

I glanced towards the corner where Fara Aden, my Somali boy — still in my service, by the way — had his sleeping-place. Fara was awake too; I could see in the faint starlight that he had raised himself on his elbow. I nodded, and with noiseless movements we made ready to go out. While I was making sure that my rifle was in order I heard the lion again; the roaring suggested that he had turned and gone off in another direction.

Outside, it had become silent all at once; the tropical night was holding its breath, waiting for the sun. The stars were paling, the air had grown thinner. The black velvet curtain had been replaced by a dark, steel-gray silk veil which might be swept aside at any moment by the breaking of day.

Fara and I set off towards the line of rocks from which the last roar had come. But we had not gone many steps before the miracle happened. A red flame spurted up behind the rocks to eastward, and against the fiery background there stood out the silhouette of a splendid male lion, striding towards the rocks slowly, with head erect, to seek there a well-earned rest after the night's exertions. He did not honor us poor human reptiles with a look; he carried his admirably proportioned body with

"LIONS DON'T CLIMB TREES"

LIONS FIND A SHOT ZEBRA

majestic strength and dignity — the King of Beasts.

"*Piga, bwana, simba!*" Fara whispered, and I knew very well that it meant: "Shoot, master, lion!" But I could not. The rifle remained under my arm.

One could not shoot a vision like that to pieces.

When I first came to Africa people used to shoot lions at night from what is called a *boma*, a sort of shelter made of thorny branches, in which the hunter sat well protected against attacks from animals. The only risk to which one was exposed was that of being killed by the stench of the putrefying carcasses which were used to attract the lions. It was a rather unsportsmanlike form of shooting, which fortunately soon fell into disrepute among African hunters. Now all shooting is forbidden between sunset and sunrise, but there was a period between these two stages when a self-respecting hunter could find an opportunity of getting in a shot at a lion at night without using a *boma*. One killed a zebra for bait, sat down by the carcass with one's rifle, and waited.

It is of one of these nights that I write. I had learned from the natives that there was a fine male lion in the neighborhood, and although I had only that one night at my disposal, I decided to make an attempt. I had rocks behind me, a spring in front, and between me and it — about five yards away — lay the zebra.

I am not exactly what is called afraid of the dark, but I do not deny that a certain percentage of my boldness disappears with the daylight. It was an unusually dark night, with thick clouds, and I had not been sitting there long before rain began to pour. In five minutes I was like a drowned rat; cooling streams tickled my spine; there was a splashing noise as soon as I moved a limb, the night cold began to penetrate my marrow, and it was as dark as the inside of a black sack. Cursing my idiotic idea — and all male lions into the bargain — I reckoned that I had at least half a dozen night hours of the same kind before me.

After two hours of tropical rain, at last something happened. First I heard the characteristic trampling of lions' paws on the drenched ground, and, that there might be no misunderstanding, the scratching sound was followed by a loud, clear roar only a few yards from my right ear.

I beg your pardon — are there two of you? Yes, four pairs of paws were moving down to the spring, about ten yards from my feet. The lion as a rule

LIONS

drinks slowly, but long. I was prepared to have to wait a good time, but this got on my nerves; did they mean to drain the spring to the last drop? At last! Now they were licking their lips loudly and with relish, as they took a few uncertain steps in my direction. I could clearly hear the air being drawn in through their nostrils when they snuffed — of course I could not see them. My heart had leaped to my throat; I was afraid.

But nothing happened. I was not to experience, for the moment at any rate, what it feels like to have a lion's body across one's neck and five times four claws plus a few fangs through one's skin.

The strongest part of the third act of the drama was its dialogue. The two lions moved off a few hundred yards nearer the back of the stage and began to talk. They roared their replies and made a deafening noise. I was once daring enough to assert that no music can be more beautiful than the roaring of a lion in the wilds of Africa. But I should really have preferred any other kind of music imaginable just then — and it seemed as if it would never end. They went on roaring at each other for two whole hours; it sounded exactly like a connubial tiff.

Suddenly the conversation stopped. The rain stopped as unexpectedly as it had begun; the pall of clouds was suddenly cleft in two, and a few stars began to blink drowsily. A dark shadow stole right up to the dead zebra. Rifle to shoulder, a shot, a flash which lit up the scene for a hundredth part of a second. But the shot was directly followed by a roaring the like of which I have never heard, either before or since. The leonine conversation just before was a mild zephyr in comparison with this thunder-clap, which might have foretold an earthquake.

The epilogue of the drama was near, however the play was to end. I dared not lower my rifle to reload the first barrel — and it was a bit of luck for me that I did not. I saw the outline of a lion's head in movement and discharged the second barrel.

Dead silence. I reloaded swiftly and mechanically. The darkness thickened again. I listened. The crickets again raised their fiddle-like voices, the hyena called his mate far away. Had I really fired, or was it a dream? A dream. . . .

The birds' song at gray of dawn woke me. Nervous strain and weariness had claimed their due. I had fallen asleep where I sat, when all around me suddenly became quiet. But now I clearly remembered the events of the night and sprang up to see what had happened.

On my side of the zebra lay a lion with the most

beautiful black mane I have ever seen — stone dead. He had received my bullet in his shoulder and died instantaneously. Across him — with hind legs on one side of his body and forelegs on the other, ready to spring — the lioness, his mate, lay stiff and cold. But so true to life was her attitude that if her tongue had not hung far out of her mouth, I should have thought her ready to attack at any moment to avenge her spouse.

She had defied death and peril without an instant's hesitation, though she knew very well that a few lithe bounds in the opposite direction would have saved her.

This wonderful feminine courage recalls to my memory — I make no comparisons, of course — another episode which also happened some years ago. During the war I was acting as a scout on the Tanganyika front, and on one occasion it became necessary to move off in haste. It was impossible to take the whole camp with us at once; I hurried on ahead, while Tanne, my wife, took command of the transport wagon, drawn by sixteen oxen, which was to follow rather more slowly.

On the third evening, just as they were preparing to pitch camp, there was a fearful disturbance among the oxen, which had been left quite alone for a few moments. Tanne hurried up and saw two lions, each of which had jumped on an ox's back. It need not be said that the teamsters had disappeared like phantoms, and my wife faced the two lions alone and unarmed, for, through an oversight, the rifles had been carefully stowed away among the baggage. But she had the heavy stockwhip, and with it she literally whipped the lions away from the oxen.

My wife made light of the incident.

"What else could I do?" she asked. "If I'd had a gun I'd have used it, of course; but the stockwhip isn't to be despised, as you see."

One of the oxen had been so severely mauled by the lion in those few seconds that it died of its wounds, but my wife's care succeeded in saving the life of the other.

It is not only peaceable oxen, however, that the lion attacks in this manner. I remember that once in the Tanga hills, when I was out shooting with a countryman of mine, we were crossing a valley when we suddenly heard a tremendous crashing and bellowing in the forest. Next moment a herd of about fifty buffaloes came thundering out from among the trees. We had to leap aside in order not to be crushed to pulp under the buffaloes' hoofs, and then we discovered the cause of the panic: on the back of the largest buffalo — a regular giant —

LIONS

rode a lion, with his claws round the buffalo's throat and his teeth in its neck. The Swede shot the lion, and in a way I thought this was a pity, for otherwise a rather strange battle between the king of beasts and one of the most dreaded of his vassals would certainly have been fought out on the open ground at the edge of the forest. Do not ask me whom I should have backed as winner. Although the lion had won the first round, it is not at all certain that he would have won the last.

Simba, the lion, is a creature of night and the plain, but he has no objection to any rock caves, copses, and undergrowth the plain may afford, where he can rest by day after his night's " work." He has no need to over-exert himself; the herds of gazelles, antelopes, and zebras that roam the endless African plains constitute his ample store of food; he has only to take what he wants. Ravenous as his appetite is, he need never be afraid of having to crawl to his lair hungry in the small hours.

He lives, on the whole, a pleasant family life. He contents himself as a rule with one wife at a time, but sometimes changes his mate. During the mating season His and Her Majesty go in company, and the family usually keep together till the cubs are grown up — thirteen or fourteen months. One often meets groups of four, five, or more animals; but old male lions with bad teeth usually live a solitary life.

It is sad, but not much is left of the old-time romance of the lion. The screen has destroyed it. I need only mention the name Serengeti for the reader to understand what I mean. Imagine an immense plain of eleven thousand square miles, which absolutely swarms with game on a fantastic scale. A large part of the fauna of Africa is represented here. I do not exaggerate if I say that over a million animals of different kinds can be seen from certain viewpoints: and the whole of this vast area has been a sanctuary since the beginning of 1936.

Practically all moving-picture films of African big game are made here. Hoeffler's *Africa Speaks*, Martin Johnson's *Simba*, and all Maxwell's excellent animal pictures have their origin in Serengeti. The lions have not merely grown accustomed to movie cameras — rather as my Kom became a household pet at the saw-mill — but have come to like both them and the men who manipulate them. It is a case of " cupboard love." Simba has become accustomed to having food thrown to him from the cameramen's cars, and as soon as he hears the sound of a motor he hurries joyfully to meet it wagging his tail, I was just going to say. The buzzing car with the cloud of dust behind it no longer means fire-spitting tubes saying "Bang-bang!" but a magnificent banquet for which he need not so much as lift a paw. And what do the kind gentlemen ask him to do in return? Pose for a moment or two in front of the blinking eye in the box. Not much to ask, is it?

I have fed Simba with meat from a car with my own hands.

I shall never forget an incident in 1935, when I was traveling through these regions with a party of Americans. We had pitched camp in the morning, and it included a real kitchen, with every modern convenience. About three o'clock in the afternoon the cook came rushing in with his hair standing on end and reported that a lion had come into the kitchen. What was he to do? Should he drive it away?

"Give Simba food and he'll go when he's had enough," I advised. And Simba did. But afterwards that lion followed our party as faithfully as a watchdog — and was never more than a hundred yards away from us. One should never be astonished at anything — nowadays! Early one morning I found four lions standing quenching their thirst in the bath in which I was going to have a dip. They went on drinking, slowly and deliberately, without taking the least notice of me. One of them looked up at me with a slightly compassionate glance, as much as to say: "Wait a bit and we'll see if there's any left for you. There's so damned little water in this region, you know, that one must take every chance one gets." As a matter of fact there was not much water left for me. But it was just enough to sit down in.

Yes, that is what Serengeti is like. But Africa is large, and in other places Simba is still true to the classic picture we have formed of him. There he still ravages the herds and makes certain roads and regions unsafe for human beings. It is in these regions that lions are hunted, and lion-hunting demands coolness, good trackers, and a sure eye. A wounded lion is, in my opinion, one of the most dangerous animals in the world. Like the great cat he is, he can make himself practically invisible even in short grass. He crouches ready to spring, and the attack comes with almost incredible swiftness. He kills, too, in the cat's way; he strikes his victim to the ground with one heavy blow of his paw, and then stops for a moment and looks round, as though considering the next step. There have been cases in which a revolver, drawn at the last second with lightning rapidity, has saved the hunter's life.

LIONS

One of my neighbors, Colonel Gray, was the chief actor in one of the most marvelous escapes of which I have ever heard. He had sworn a feud against Simba for the simple reason that the lions could not be induced to leave his cattle in peace. Time after time the old man — Gray was sixty-five — postponed the execution of his resolve, but one morning, when he found that the four-legged robbers had killed his best heifer, he felt that the cup was full to overflowing. The colonel built himself a platform in a tree near one of the cattle-folds and began his watch an hour after nightfall.

Hour after hour passed without any of the robber band showing themselves. But just when the colonel had half decided to give it up, he caught sight of three creeping shadows moving in the direction of the fold. Criminals! He fired at all three of them, but in the darkness he was not sure of the result and resolved to await the dawn, which could not be far off.

In the first dim light of day he clambered down to the ground and found that he had killed two of the lions on the spot, while the third — from all indications badly wounded — had withdrawn to some brushwood. As the trail of blood showed plainly the route the beast had taken, the colonel decided to follow it up.

AFRICAN HUNTER

He did not need to search long; the lion was waiting for him and attacked him. Gray fired as the beast sprang, but did not hit it exactly where he meant to; the animal leaped on him, and so began a hand-to-hand fight which recalls Samson's Biblical contest with the lion. Two seconds later the colonel found himself disarmed; the lion tore the rifle out of his hand and flung it aside. Then it dug its teeth into the colonel's right hand and positively led its prey off towards the neighboring brushwood to make an end of him. The colonel, worn out by loss of blood and his exertions — as he himself told me next day — had no choice but reluctantly to go with the lion to the death which awaited him. But they had taken only a few steps when he felt the grip on his right hand weaken — and the lion fell to the ground dead. The last bullet had finally done its work.

Luckily Arusha hospital was only a few miles away, but as telephone and ambulance are still unknown luxuries in the depths of Africa, the colonel — despite the shock to his nerves, the loss of blood, and the horrible pain in his hand — had himself to drive his Ford to the hospital, an achievement which bears eloquent testimony to the coolness and presence of mind of this man of sixty-five. After a bare month's detention he was discharged from

LIONS

hospital, and in memory of the event he adorned one of his walls with the rifle, in the butt of which the lion's broken teeth had lodged. He also framed the story of Samson's duel with the lion (Judges xiv) and hung it up under the trophy.

VI. *"Good, Dangerous Sport"*

LION-HUNTING on horseback in Africa is first-class sport.

A lion pursued is extremely fast for a few hundred yards, but quickly gets winded, and if the pursuer continues his advance, it waits for him behind some bush or in long grass, ready to attack in self-defense. You must therefore always keep an eye on your quarry. If you are not sure where the lion is, you may easily ride straight on to it, and that is the end of the business — one spring and you are wounded or killed.

A gallop over rough country is a real joy, and when one has to keep one's eye on two or three lions at the same time and knows that a mistake

"GOOD, DANGEROUS SPORT"

means fairly certain death, the gallop is a good deal more exciting than a ride round the Park.

The first time I had a chance of taking part in an adventure of this kind was in January 1914, when the American multimillionaire Paul Rainey, through the well-known white hunter, the Austrian, Fritz Schindeler, invited my wife and me to join a hunt which he intended to arrange in the Kedong valley, not far from Naivasha, where my uncle then had a farm. We waited vainly for three days for the guide who was to come and conduct us to their camp, and then returned to Nairobi, where we heard the sad news that a misadventure such as I have indicated above had happened to Schindeler. He had kept his eye on the fleeing lion and had not noticed another, which had leaped at him and dragged him from his horse. He was now lying in the hospital, still alive, but with no hope of recovery, for the lion had torn out a large part of his intestines.

He had seen me off by train only a few days before, when I was going to meet my wife, and had given me a word of warning. "Look here, Blixen," he had said, "remember always to be careful with lions. They'll get you one fine day."

A week later he himself had been killed.

As I am writing of hunting on horseback, I can

assure my readers that it is always interesting and exciting.

I have often hunted in Kenya with the well-known polo player Winston Guest. The last time he was out in Africa, his special ambition was to ride down buffalo, and he brought five thoroughbred horses for this purpose. We hired some twenty pack-horses in addition and went to Uaso-Nyiro, not far from Rumuruti. Here there are buffalo in fairly open country, but the ground is rocky and broken by many ravines.

The first day we were out — Winston, Raymond Hook, and I — the first thing we came across was a large wart-hog. We had no spears with us, but took up the pursuit nevertheless, and after a swift gallop over rough ground we brought the animal to bay. When we approached, it attacked Winston's horse, but a quick shot from his Colt revolver brought it down with a broken neck.

A little farther on we sighted some thirty buffaloes grazing in a meadow on the other side of a ravine. We made our way down into the valley, stumbled upon a game track there, and gradually approached our still unsuspecting buffaloes. We gave them two hundred yards' start and then off we went. Nothing can be more exciting than a gallop like that — bellowings at intervals, bushes

CAMERA HUNTERS APPRECIATE THE RHINOCEROS

THREE-HORNED RHINOCEROS, SHOT IN 1932

"GOOD, DANGEROUS SPORT"

that nearly fling one off one's horse — the whole in a reeking cloud of dust. To fire is impossible, to photograph equally so. There is just the joy of pursuing and seeing what it is like.

Our buffaloes knew the ground well and were soon in thick brushwood, into which we could not follow them. So we let the horses rest a bit before we returned to camp, but after we had walked them for half an hour we came upon seven more buffaloes. Another breakneck gallop, which ended in the same way as the first. Unfortunately we received news that day by aeroplane that Guest's mother had fallen ill at Nairobi, and we had to return at once. But I hope some day to have an opportunity of making a fresh attempt and surprising the buffaloes in open country, where no protecting brushwood will deprive us at the last moment of the triumph of stopping them.

In his book *The Man-Eaters of Tsavo* Colonel Patterson describes how he got the better of two lions which had some sixty human lives on their consciences. I quote from his book an example which shows strikingly how incalculable Simba can be when he is taken that way.

When the railway from Mombasa to Lake Victoria was under construction, four engineers were housed in a first-class railway car which had been driven on to a siding at Tsavo. They had turned two compartments into sleepers, so that both upper and lower berths were in use. Doors and windows were, of course, wide open all night; nevertheless one of the engineers, who was in the compartment nearest the door, thought it was getting too hot in the car; so he took his pillow, mattress, and sheet and made up his bed on the platform.

In the middle of the night one of the man-eaters appeared, stepped carefully over the snoring man on the platform, climbed up into the corridor, went past the first compartment, the door of which stood open, went into the other, stood up on the man who was lying in the lower berth, seized the poor devil in the upper berth, and jumped out of the window with him. Why him rather than any of the others? Now, can anyone explain it? But in any case the two mass murderers' cup was full; Patterson shot them both soon after.

One often hears in snake stories that people have saved themselves from bites that meant certain death by remaining absolutely motionless. The principle can be applied to lions too, as the following episode shows. During my earliest years in Africa I was riding from Gil Gil to Rumuruti to

"GOOD, DANGEROUS SPORT"

meet my wife. The road, which has now been transformed into a well-macadamized motor-road, was then a wretched natives' track, which compelled one to maintain a very moderate speed and calculate one's stages carefully. Luckily I had my old friend Kolbe on whom I could inflict myself the first night. Kolbe was occupied in surveying this region for the State and had his headquarters in an insignificant little grass hut close to the track. But when I arrived I did not know where I was for the moment. Kolbe's hut had not looked like that when I was there last. It had grown higher, and when I entered I found Kolbe in a bedroom on the first floor, which had not existed on my previous visit.

Kolbe smiled at my astonished face.

"Don't you like my skyscraper?" he said.

I had to admit that the new style of the house — from a purely architectural point of view — did not particularly appeal to me. Kolbe grew serious all of a sudden.

"As you know, one has to put æsthetic considerations aside sometimes," he said. "Take a chair, if you can find one, and sit down, and I'll tell you all about it. Excuse my not being able to run about and wait on you, but I've got a bit of a scratch on my thigh."

I gradually began to put two and two together. And I missed Rip, Kolbe's faithful terrier.

"Yes," he went on, "Rip has been gone since one day last week — one can build grass skyscrapers at American speed, and one can lose a faithful friend just as quickly.

"It was a dark night when it happened; I was in bed in my old room down below with the lamp lighted, turned down, and I had gone to sleep with my spectacles on.

"And perhaps that was lucky. For when I woke up an hour or two later, I saw in an instant what was happening; a lioness was staring right into my face, and she had my poor Rip's body in her mouth. The thing that mattered now was to control my muscles; the slightest movement would have meant death. The lioness laid the dog on the floor and continued to gaze at me. I managed to remain absolutely motionless; my eyelids quivered, but I was able by a great effort to prevent myself from blinking. I have no idea how long this lasted — to me it was an eternity. At last she picked the dog up again, and then I flung myself out of bed — on the wall side. I thought I had been quick, but the lioness was quicker. She struck like lightning and ripped up my thigh — look here!"

To judge from the bandage, it must have been

a bad tear; the whole leg was swathed from the top to a little way below the knee.

"Then she went off with Rip," Kolbe continued. "But the next evening, just at twilight, as I was sitting at the door with my damaged leg on one chair, a whisky on another, and my gun on my knees, I saw last night's marauder come stealing towards the house. I needn't tell you I took good aim! Rip was avenged — but that doesn't prevent my poor leg from hurting damnably. Still, I shall sleep a little more securely on the first floor in the future."

The market value of a shot lion is not great, but although the skin is not quoted in the fur market, the hunter is always glad to get it. It is not so easy as it looks to skin a lion, but there are many clever, well-trained skinners among the blacks. The whole thing must be done in proper order; one single false cut can ruin the whole skin. But after the first scientific cuts along the center of the belly and down the legs, the body is not difficult to flay. The claws and head, on the other hand, require both patience and skill. Two or three trained skinners can skin a beast in half an hour. Then the skin is salted, aired, folded up, and packed. The body is left to the vultures.

But the lion's fat is carefully preserved. It has

an established reputation as a remedy for rheumatic pains. There may be something in it. I myself, fortunately, have never needed to test its power to ease pain. The blacks melt down the fat and bottle it. The price of a bottle varies from ninepence to half a crown, and an average lion yields about fifteen bottles.

So it cannot be said that a man goes lion-hunting for love of gain.

VII. *Rhinoceros and Other Game*

ONE can make money out of a shot rhinoceros. In the first place, it has its horn, which the Chinese medicine-men are eager to obtain; this, when pulverized, is an important ingredient in a preparation for the curing of sexual weakness which is said to have a tremendous sale among the native gentlemen in Peking, Shanghai, and Canton. Thirty shillings a pound is a fairly steady quotation for rhinoceros horns, and as a horn can weigh more than twelve or fourteen pounds, it is not hard to understand how sought after they are.

Secondly, rhinoceros hide can be used for quite a variety of purposes. The skin is practically wearproof. And, third and last, the blacks like the meat and will pay a good price for it. A slain rhinoceros, in short, represents a small fortune.

And the rhinoceros has one characteristic in common with capital — he does not occur in alarming quantities; he may, indeed, be said to be rare. In comparison with the elephant he is very scantily represented, and the area in which he occurs is much more limited. The fears of his extermination which have been expressed are perhaps not altogether unreasonable — he is much more easily killed than the elephant by both white and black hunters; but the Game Department is keeping its eye on the danger, and it may be hoped that the protective measures taken are proving efficacious.

The rhinoceros is the living tank. When he rolls forward to the assault, every live thing in his way is crushed — and he is the only animal which invariably attacks when threatened by sudden danger. He unconsciously plays upon the terror evoked by his unexpected thundering charge through the bush. The experienced white hunter is perhaps not so easily frightened, but one can never be sure that the blacks will not fling down their burdens headlong and take to their heels when the rhinoceros comes thundering towards them like a snorting locomotive.

If it happens to be one's own porters who are the objects of the rhinoceros's attentions, good-by to the valuable contents of the whisky-bottle! Everything that can be smashed is smashed when the loads are flung recklessly to the ground.

Perhaps, all things considered, the comparison to a tank or a locomotive is not really the right one. The tank is guided by a reasoning brain, and the locomotive follows its track, but the rhinoceros simply blazes ahead. He neither hears nor sees. I remember one day when my friend Cooper and I were stealing along a path trying to get near two lions. We were thinking of nothing but the lions, and the whole of our attention was directed to the avoidance of the slightest noise which could put them on their guard.

Chuff — chuff — chuff . . . and a crashing like a broadside from a battleship — a rhinoceros was on us. We both of us naturally jumped out of the way — and pretty quick too — but, all the same, the beast got his horn under the strap of Cooper's glasses. Not that the rhinoceros troubled about that! I doubt if he even noticed that he had taken Cooper in tow; at any rate, there was nothing to show it. Luckily for Cooper, the strap broke at once, so that he was not carried any farther, but who knows what might not have happened if it had been a first-class strap? I dared not fire for fear of hitting my old friend.

Another rhinoceros incident is just as fresh in my memory. Alfred Vanderbilt was the chief actor on that occasion, and heaven knows who would have become entitled to the Vanderbilt millions if a certain rhinoceros had been a bit quicker. We were at the time — it was early evening — out after nothing more dangerous than guinea-fowl. I had just shot a pair with my short-range practice rifle and sent two of our gun-bearers to pick up these valuable additions to our rather monotonous bill of fare, when one of our black boys began to shout and yell:

"Look out, look out, sir!"

Then I saw. Two rhinoceroses were making straight for us at a jog-trot. My practice rifle was loaded, but that was of no use to me. I might as well have let off a pea-shooter at them. The gun-bearer had taken my proper rifle when he went to pick up the guinea-fowl. I shouted and waved my hat to make the beasts alter course. No good. Stronger measures had to be applied; I rushed to the gun-bearer, snatched my rifle, and blazed away. The rhinoceroses altered course at once; but so had Vanderbilt, and I saw him disappear unarmed into the brushwood for which the rhinoceroses were now making in single file.

For all his millions Vanderbilt could not in that crucial moment purchase his life, which really hung upon the cheap bullet in my rifle. I fired, and one rhinoceros fell stone dead scarcely two yards from Vanderbilt's heels. The other, terrified by his companion's fate, turned about and vanished in a cloud of dust. The whole affair was a matter of thirty seconds, and when it was over we could not help laughing.

I do not think the rhinoceros kills for the pleasure of it. His hereditary instinct bids him attack when he thinks that danger threatens, and if this categorical imperative sometimes ends disastrously for the man concerned, it may just as often turn out badly for the rhinoceros himself. The rhinoceros, for example, which charged the engine of the Uganda train realized his mistake too late.

There is one class of hunters with which the rhinoceros is very popular — those who hunt with the camera. The animal's hearing is bad and his sight even worse, so that it is easy to take close-up pictures of him in very natural attitudes. Certainly he has a good ally in the tick-birds, small birds which live on ticks and sit on the rhinoceros's back. When any danger threatens they first set up their sharp warning cry: " chi-chi-chi," and if the menace comes nearer they leave him. So the first thing the camera hunter has to do is to outwit the tickbirds, and this is by no means impossible if one brings one's intelligence to bear on it.

As it has never been my intention to write a zoological text-book, I will deal briefly with the rest of the African fauna. The parts in which game is most plentiful are the great plains of Kenya, Tanganyika, and Uganda and certain districts of Northern Rhodesia. Game is abundant right up to the latitude of Lake Chad, but not even the desert is without representatives of the antelope and gazelle tribes. These animals exist for a large part of the year completely without water, and not a blade of grass is to be seen in the regions where the oryx antelopes live. They sustain themselves on sand burrs plus the scanty vegetation they can discover here and there, but despite this incredibly meager bill of fare the specimens I have succeeded in shooting had a layer of fat between the skin and the flesh — which I have never found in any buck killed in regions where there is a more ample food supply. The explanation of this phenomenon I leave to the professors; the fact is as stated. The lard is probably intended by nature to serve as a kind of iron ration for hard times, but how can it be formed with the material available?

Nature! Nowhere in the world, I think, does the hunter come into such close contact with her as in East Africa, and nowhere on the surface of the globe are such triumphs of adaptability to be seen. Africa is the land of violent contrasts. The heat of the tropics and the cold of the north, the desert drought and the floods of the rainy season intersect one another as though following lines drawn by an architect's ruler, but the beasts make themselves at home everywhere. The fauna merges itself in its surroundings and regulates its minor needs and its way of life accordingly, with an incredible pliability. Elephant and buffalo seek salt on the ocean beaches as readily as from the soda deposits on the mountain slopes right up to the snow-line; lion and leopard delight both coast-dweller and inland farmer with their music by night. The same francolins (a kind of partridge) breed as well in the dry scrub of the lower regions as among the trees of the high plateaus: and you can fill the pot with guinea-fowl all over Africa, from the Cape to the Sahara.

The plain fauna consists mainly of zebras, gazelles, and antelopes. The zebra is usually found in large herds, multitudes, thousands; and among them may be seen Thomson's gazelles, impalas, and Grant's gazelles in several forms.

Gnu occur commonly in East Africa, but are not now found farther west. The hartebeest is common in its many different forms, along with its cousin, the topi. Of all these animals the gazelle is the prettiest, the hartebeest (or kongoni, as it is also called) the ugliest, the wildebeest or gnu the most grotesque, but perhaps the most impressive when seen in the mass. It reminds one a little of the awe-inspiring bison of the old American children's books. When God had created all the animals, the legend runs, there were a number of spare parts left over, and as his economical instinct forbade him to let anything be wasted, he put together that curious beast the gnu.

The largest of the antelopes is the eland, which recalls our northern cattle. It has always been well protected by the game laws, and is, moreover, by nature shy and hard to approach. The eland occurs in two different forms — the commoner Cape eland on the eastern plains and Lord Derby's eland in Central Africa. Lord Derby's eland is rather larger, has longer horns, and has eleven pale stripes along the body. The eland has as a rule strong and well-developed horns, a result of the practical use to which it puts them — it uses them to pull down trees so as to get at the young twigs, which it regards as a great delicacy. Lord Derby's antelope is exceedingly shy; outstanding sporting qualities are demanded of the man who would bring it down.

The animal which most resembles Lord Derby's eland is the kudu — undoubtedly the prettiest of African antelopes, with its silver-gray color, white stripes, noble head, large ears, velvety eyes, and spiral horns. The kudu occurs in two forms, the greater and the lesser kudu, always in scrub and most often preferring hilly ground. Other forms which inhabit similar country are the sable and roan antelopes, the bushbuck, several forms of duikers, the steinbuck, and the smallest of them all, the dik-dik.

In the great forests we find — largest of all — the stately bongo, another antelope with horns as twisted as the bushbuck's, but more suggesting the eland. The bongo is dark brown with white diagonal stripes and is particularly difficult of access on account of the ground it inhabits. There are few white hunters who have killed it with their own hand. In the depths of the forests we find, too, the very rare okapi, a woodland species of the giraffe tribe.

Nor is the African wild pig to be despised as a quarry. Hunting wild pig on horseback and finishing the gallop with a duel with the far from harmless beast is good sport. The pig occurs for the most part on the plain and in scrub; the giant black forest hog is found — as the name indicates — only in the great forests. The red and gray long-haired bush-hogs are varieties, too, for which it is worth while to wear out a pair of hunting-boots.

CHEETAH WITH ITS PREY

Photo, G. Prud
NATURE AND ART: RHINOCEROS AND AN AEROPLAN

VIII. *Cooper*

A HUNTING expedition in Africa calls for much thoughtful preparation, careful planning, and organization. I have guided many hunters through the country, but the one who is most firmly enshrined in my memory is my friend Cooper.

Major A. F. Cooper, an English gentleman, engaged me in 1927 for a three months' safari and asked me to meet him at Mombasa. I realized almost immediately that we should get on well — and it was no false prophecy. After nearly ten years of hardships endured together and many bottles of whisky shared, I dare to affirm that we are the best friends in the world. Though he did have an insane notion the first evening we discussed the plan of campaign — he had got an idea into his head of leaving his gun at home and killing his game with bow and arrows. This was the conception of an American who was trying to persuade people that it was not gentlemanly to go out shooting with a gun — it was not fair to the wild beasts, if you please! And I had no little difficulty in persuading Cooper to give up his bow — at any rate till after his first meeting with a lion — but at last I succeeded.

After a few days' preparation at Mombasa we went off by car along the old caravan road to Voi railway station, where we were to dine and spend the night. We shouted for our newly engaged cook, Musa, but he was nowhere to be found. Closer investigation revealed that he had tumbled off the truck; some of the boys recollected that he had been there for at least half the journey, but had then disappeared.

"Why didn't you call out, you idiots?" cried Cooper, exasperated and hungry.

Well, that was a question no one could answer. Musa was a superior person, and if he chose to disappear suddenly, it was perfectly in order.

What was to be done? Should we drive back and pick up the cook or let him fend for himself and prepare our own dinner? Our aching bones led us to choose the second alternative, and it was a good thing we did, for in the middle of dinner Musa turned up. It was true that he had been flung off the truck at a bend, but he came down in a sitting position and did not even feel a tender spot anywhere. He had run after us for a while, but when he suddenly heard the noise of an approaching train puffing up a hill, he hurried to the railroad track close by, climbed on to a buffer of one of the rearmost cars, and rode on it to Voi — a smart bit of work. Afterwards, too, the boy showed himself enterprising and quick. He was with me for several years.

We left Voi next day. Our route led us by Moshi, in Tanganyika, at the foot of Kilimanjaro, whose glacier-covered top, over eighteen thousand feet high, is a shining landmark hundreds of miles away. Before Moshi we saw and drove past masses of game, but immediately after, we stopped for lunch in oppressive heat under the mountain's snow-cap.

In the evening we reached Arusha, where the rest of the expedition joined us, and early next morning we started with the truck and a four-wheeled cart, drawn by twelve donkeys and driven by a Boer named Neil. Musa, the cook, two boys, and ten porters formed the crew of the truck, and after a further two days' travel we had the first stage behind us; the district was rich in game, and hunting could begin.

That same evening we shot two zebras as bait for lions, put them down in a suitable place, and as accompaniment to our evening drink we had the sweetest music we could have desired: lions were roaring against each other in the neighborhood of our zebras. As soon as it grew light — perhaps a little before — we were on our legs and creeping towards the bait. Four lions were eating till their jaws creaked, but their hour had not yet come. Let them first eat their fill and seek their lair in the neighboring brushwood, and then we would send beaters to stir them up; we should get better sport that way.

Breakfast in camp was glorious; our appetite was as good as that of the lions outside, and the thought of the coming hunt thrilled us. At eleven o'clock we went out and reconnoitered the ground. The four lions were sleeping soundly and heavily in the depths of the brushwood. The boys were instructed as to how they should go forward and, by shouting and throwing stones, drive the animals towards the exit where Cooper and I had taken up our position.

It was not many minutes before the grayish-yellow muzzle of a lioness appeared; she snuffed and gazed round and next moment moved on — towards us. Behind her appeared her mate, creeping very slowly out of the brushwood, and behind him again lion number three, followed by a lioness. Number three was one of the finest beasts I have ever seen.

"Take the third first," I whispered to Cooper, and the next second came the report of his rifle. An angry roar announced that the bullet had found its mark; the second shot followed, which also was an evident hit. But none of the animals were lying dead — they all four disappeared into the same brushwood from which they had come. We did not have to search long for number three — the beast lay crumpled up, as dead as the stone behind which it had fallen — but of number two only the track of blood was to be seen.

Now was the rub. First, the whole strength of the camp was mobilized, a chain was formed, and the encirclement began. It was not long before the wounded lion was located; it had chosen a very thick patch of brushwood in a slight depression, on the farther side of which was a tall tree. We tried throwing stones, firing blank cartridges, and shouting — in vain. An angry growling told us that the gentleman in question did not intend to appear.

Then I sent in our donkeys, but that was no use at all. A fresh roar sent them galloping back to the camp in wild panic. The situation was undeniably difficult. It would have been suicide to creep right up to the lion among the thick thorn bushes, but, on the other hand, a wounded animal cannot be left to its fate.

Then I proposed to Neil that he should climb up into the tall tree on the far side of the lion's place of refuge and see if he could get a sight of the lion from it. Like the Boer he was, he went up without hesitation, but he had not got half-way to the top before the lion was after him. There were a few rather nasty seconds. The beast's claws were not six inches beneath his feet when I fired my first shot. The bullet hit the lion in the breast, but did not kill him. Then he turned on me like a madly sputtering giant rocket. The bullet from my second barrel entered his mouth at a distance of five feet, and he rolled over dead at my feet.

" Well, my dear Cooper," I said, " what about your bow and arrows now? "

" Hm! " Cooper replied, as he wiped the sweat from his forehead, " I think the bow and arrows had better stay where they are. It's good enough fun with a rifle. And quite sporting enough."

Next day we continued our journey. I drove on ahead early with the truck to look for a suitable camping-ground, taking with me Juma Nandi, my gun-bearer, a good, capable lad, and a couple of boys. We found a pretty good place, and when we had unloaded our things I told Juma to follow the bed of the river, which was dried up in places, till he found drinking-water. Then I got into the car and drove back to our old camp to fetch Cooper and the others. But when we reached the new camping-ground at lunch-time, Juma was not there. The boys said that he had not been seen since he went out at my orders to search for water. I had to do as the mother did who sent her little boy to the village for milk — go after him and fetch both the boy and the milk. When I had got a little way up the dry river-bed I heard Juma's whistling. He had climbed up to the top of a tree, and shouted that eight lions were lying and crouching among the bushes under the tree.

"One of them has been half-way up after me three times," he called. "You'd better bring as many guns and as many men as you can."

Juma was right — as many guns and as many men as I could. Cooper and I went off at the head of a small party armed with all the rifles the camp possessed and carrying saucepan lids, frying-pans, empty gasolene-cans, water-buckets — in other words, everything which could possibly be used to make a noise with. Our first task was to free poor Juma, who had already spent four or five hours up the tree.

The party advanced, making a deafening noise. There was roaring and growling from the long grass in front of us, but the enemy retreated. Neil and the cook celebrated a regular orgy of hideous noise; the light of victory shone in their eyes, and step by step we advanced till our semicircular front had driven the lions back into the thick brushwood behind the tree. Juma was then released from his imprisonment amid cheers.

As things now were, there was nothing to be done but wait for twilight, when the lions would leave the brushwood and come out into the open of their own accord. We waited in the most profound silence. Five o'clock came and another half-hour passed. Then a twig snapped suddenly in the brushwood, and a few leaves rustled, although there was absolutely no wind. Breathless excitement. Then one of the lions stepped out, yawned, and stretched itself lazily in the last rays of the evening sun. The other seven followed slowly and grouped themselves in picturesque attitudes as though in a photographer's studio.

"It was that one went for me," Juma whispered in my ear, pointing to a fine male lion with a beautiful black mane.

The lion got a bullet in his shoulder at about a hundred yards' range, leaped into the air and was dead. The others galloped away across the plain, and we let them disappear, as it was presumably the lion with the black mane that was prone to attack human beings. Three lions in two days was not so bad, either.

As to the reason why the eight lions absolutely refused to leave their refuge in this particular patch of undergrowth, I have no theory to offer. There was no water, no carcasses, the brushwood was quite close to the track, and there were a thousand other hiding-places in the neighborhood which would have served their purpose much better. But, as I have already observed, there is an incalculable strain in the lion's mentality which defies logical analysis on the part of the hunter.

I may mention that ten blacks at least have been attacked, carried off, and devoured by lions at this very place. The Government, very rightly, has put up a notice: "Beware of lions!" A most excellent guide for lion-hunters! My only fear is that the notice is out of date — for six months later I shot two lions just under the board itself, and subsequent searches have revealed that no more marauders have been there since. So I presume that Cooper and I made a clean sweep.

Next day we drove along the foot of the Essimingor mountain chain to the western slope of the Rift valley, which here rises sheer from the salt water of Lake Manjara to the M'bulu plateau. There is plenty of game there — zebras, gnus, kongonis, oryx, and gazelles. We kept our eyes open in particular for oryx and buffalo, and a rhinoceros if we could find one with a fine horn. Lake Manjara, twenty-two miles long and five miles wide, contains soda, and its water is undrinkable, except at the places where rivers and brooks from the plateau flow into it. Here small delta islands of mud, with reeds and marsh plants, have been formed, a favorite resort of buffalo and hippopotamus in particular. There are plenty of birds too — masses of wild duck and coots, and the shores are pink with flamingoes for miles on end. A sportsman's El Dorado.

Early in the morning we went off to the mouth of the river, where the evening before we had discovered the spoor of two large bull buffaloes. Thousands of animals were grazing quite close to the river, of whose water they had drunk during the night. A rhinoceros — his horn, unluckily, too small for our pretensions — was just on his way home towards Essimingor, in whose thick brushwood he probably lived. Far off we saw, in the gray of dawn, a small herd of buffaloes. We turned our glasses on them, but could discover no bull, though we counted fourteen animals — cows and calves. In the long grass, however, we detected the backs of two more buffaloes, which were moving slowly towards the herd with the obvious intention of joining it; and as the wind was in our favor, we crept along the edge of the reeds in the hope of getting within range before they reached the others. We succeeded. We got a clear view of them at about a hundred and fifty yards — a fairly young bull with fine horns and an older beast with poorer headgear. Cooper fired at the former, but got a gleam of sun in his eyes, and the bullet hit too low. Both animals turned and disappeared into the marsh. After some minutes' discussion we decided to postpone the pursuit until after lunch and, instead, try to get hold of an oryx and a few duck for our larder.

The oryx — an imposing beast the size of a stag,

with long, straight horns as sharp as a gimlet, which even the lion respects — Cooper disposed of after a squirming and creeping which would have done credit to a snake-man; but the duck defied our exertions. We had to content ourselves with a little bustard.

Directly after lunch we took up the pursuit of the wounded bull buffalo. A good deal of blood was still visible on the grass, but it was dark, so it did not come from the lungs. We followed the traces, but it was a slow business. The wet ground was churned up by thousands of animals' feet; at times we sank up to our knees in it. Cooper puffed and I cursed mildly. Hush! What was that? Tick-birds. Then we could not be far from the two buffaloes. But we could see nothing for the long grass, which obstructed the view in every direction. Cooper had to climb up on my shoulders and act as a living periscope.

"Well, Cooper, what can you see?"

"Something black — and the horns of a buffalo moving, but I think it's the old one."

"We must frighten it away. Wait a moment."

With Cooper still on my shoulders, I fired a shot into the air. The effect was what I had calculated — the unwounded buffalo disappeared in a cloud of mud, and we were able to approach the wounded beast with our rifles at the ready, prepared for an attack any second. But these were superfluous measures of precaution — the buffalo was as dead as could be. His horns measured three feet ten inches. Then the cutting-up began, but we left some of the meat behind in the hope of catching a leopard at it next morning. We went to look before we started next day, but there had been no catch. And so we continued our journey.

IX. *In Craterland*

We worked slowly forward along the slope of the Rift valley to N'garuka, where we left the wagons and reorganized the expedition. The donkeys were converted from draft animals into pack animals, and a further twenty porters, engaged in advance, joined the safari. And so we went into craterland. Here there was a mass of buffalo and rhinoceros spoor, but we had not time to follow them, as we had to get to the next camping-ground — the lake by the Elanairobi crater — before dusk.

I shall never forget the dizzy sight that met my eyes when I climbed to the top of the crater and looked down into the gigantic caldron. Nearly a thousand feet below me shone the vast steely mirror of the lake, untouched by the faintest breath of air for centuries past. The slopes inside the crater were clothed with beautiful, shady woods whose luxuriant foliage was reflected in the lake. The surface of the water seemed to be strewn with thousands of pink rose-leaves, but the glass revealed what they were — gay flamingoes, swimming quietly about. Opposite me rose Lengai (God's mountain) with snow on its peak. I wished I could write poetry; as it was, I had to content myself with saying: "I have never seen anything more beautiful in my life, I could never have dreamed that anything so lovely and poetic existed on our earth." After that, it mattered nothing that the snow on God's mountain was not snow at all, but soda, for it looked exactly like snow.

Next day we proceeded at a height of 6,000 feet above sea-level and over quite tolerable ground. Great open, fertile fields, splendid pastures, with small copses planted here and there — a regular land of one's dreams, this country that was once German East Africa, which the Germans had meant for their own settlers, but England — after Versailles — handed back to the Masai.

N'goro-goro is reputed to be the world's largest crater; and without doubt it is. The flat bottom of that giant's caldron must be nearly twelve miles across; the sides are steep and you can look down into it from a height of about 600 feet. At the southern end is a small lake, but it is dried up by evaporation in the hot season. Let us descend to the plain — which means that we have climbed to a height of 4,500 feet above sea-level; this is the height of the bottom of the giant's caldron.

Two little rivers run in to east and south, and there a few pretty mimosa copses grow, but otherwise there is just one immense grass plain with an extraordinarily fertile soil.

I need not say that this plain is a paradise for grazing animals. Zebras, gazelles, and antelopes roam about in thousands, and the swamps are a favorite resort of hippopotami. How they ever found their way to this secluded spot over long waterless stretches of country is one of the unsolved puzzles of the African fauna.

And all this vast area is a sanctuary. A few years ago all hunting was forbidden, not only on the crater plain, but also within a radius of nearly six miles round its edge. At the same time a rest-house was built and a road was made, so that the public can now reach the eighth wonder of the world with no great inconvenience.

But in 1927 — when Cooper and I visited the

ZEBRAS AT THE TANA RIVER

THERE'S DANGER ABOUT

place — there were no roads in those parts, and hunting was not prohibited. Before the war a German named Ziedentopf had owned a considerable property there, had built a house and farm buildings and bred cattle on a large scale. After the war an Englishman, Sir Charles Ross, became the owner, and as I knew that he carefully preserved his game, Cooper and I had agreed that we would shoot nothing on his land — we would content ourselves with shooting with Cooper's movie camera. We pitched our camp by a crystalline spring.

When this had been done we had a look at our surroundings. A few large eucalyptus trees still flourished where the garden had once been, but otherwise the whole place presented a lamentable picture of decay and neglect. The only thing which remained fairly untouched by time was a combined hen-house and pigeon-cot in the middle of the farm.

When we approached it a magnificent male lion crawled out of the opening, gazed at us arrogantly for a second, and departed across the plain at a dignified pace. The pungent menagerie smell which issued from the hen-house told us that the king of beasts had not only used it as a casual residence, but had certainly lived there for some time. And a lion could find worse quarters; by night he hunted on the game-covered plain just outside, by day he took his rest in the shade inside the henhouse.

It was, as I have said, an unusually fine beast with a splendid mane — a first-class trophy even for a very blasé hunter. The well-kept mane also supported the presumption that the lion had lived in the hen-house a long time; creeping about among thorny undergrowth, reeds, and long grass wears out the mane, while the lodger in the henhouse had as fine a head of hair as a menagerie lion.

We followed his movements through our glasses. Without hurrying himself in the least — on the contrary, he sat down now and then and panted in the great heat — he strolled majestically across the plain, and not till he reached the top of a low ridge about three miles away did he lie down on his belly. It was impossible to detect him with the naked eye, but we succeeded with a Zeiss glass which magnified eight times, and as the lion's sight is about eight times as good as a man's, he could follow all our movements from the viewpoint he had chosen with strategic skill.

Cooper's fingers itched to set his movie camera at work, but the difficulty of getting close to the lion deterred us. The detour we should be obliged to make would take us several hours. After breakfast, however, we felt more optimistic and started for the ridge, Cooper with the movie camera and I with the rifles, while my trusty Juma had been ordered to stay in camp, keep his eyes, or rather glasses, on the lion, and signal to us with a white handkerchief when we had reached the place to which the animal had gone — if it was not still in its old place.

It took us nearly three hours to get there, walking and crawling; the perspiration streamed from our poor bodies, but when, proceeding noiselessly, with Cooper creeping hard at my heels, I reached the bush in front of which the lion had lain down, what did I find? After our tense expectation, nothing at all. I semaphored to Juma and put my glasses to my eyes. The handkerchief pointed straight ahead — so the lion had moved a short way down the ridge. And so he had; there lay His Majesty, looking straight at Juma's insane gesticulations with the handkerchief; he had not discovered us. But a stone which I threw made him move, the movie camera began to click, and I stood with my rifle ready in case of eventualities. Those were the best close-ups ever taken of a male lion — and I did not have to fire.

Next morning it was the turn of Africa's scavengers, the four-legged department — the hyenas. I willingly admit that they have many repulsive characteristics, and that there are many excellent reasons for the contempt in which they are held. They live on carrion, old rotten meat, are cowardly and treacherous by nature, and often begin to eat sick animals mercilessly without killing them first. Their howling at night may get on one's nerves, too; but if one takes the trouble to observe them rather more closely — in their family life, so to speak — one finds in them certain winning qualities.

I once had a tame hyena, which showed many attractive traits of character; she was faithful and intelligent, and more playful than any dog I have had. We played together clumsily, rolling about on the floor; and she was as fond of caresses as a spaniel.

Well, that morning Cooper and I had sat down with the camera near a water-hole, and in a little while seven hyenas appeared, with their ugly rolling walk. We had each of us crouched down behind a concealing boulder, and hoped to get a good picture of them drinking, but we got something better still — a hundred feet or two of excellent bathing pictures. As I sat there enjoying the playful creatures' antics, I could not help thinking of the story of Dr. Jekyll and Mr. Hyde. . . .

The same day we came upon a whole army of

eland on the slope of the crater, among gnus and zebras — several hundred animals at least. They were not eager for human society; as soon as we approached they withdrew timidly. But Cooper had sworn that he would get some close-up pictures of them, and the only thing to be done was to try the customary ruse. Cooper sat down to wait, well hidden, with the camera camouflaged behind a heap of stones, while I, with three of our gun-bearers, made a wide detour over the countryside so as to get behind the beasts and drive them down to the camera. It sounds simple and easy when one describes the maneuver; in practice it took more than two hours of toil and perspiration. But later we had the satisfaction of recording a great film triumph; for not only did this whole multitude of game — zebras, kongonis, gnus, eland, etc. — parade right in front of the clicking camera, but in the midst of it all two beautiful lionesses rose out of the long grass in which they had been hidden and strolled up the slope of the crater, the other beasts making way for them respectfully. There was no panic or alarm; for, in the first place, the beasts knew it was very seldom their ruler attacked in daylight, and, secondly, they felt that security which the English characterize by the expression " safety in numbers " — why should it be I, when there are so many others? Cooper took more than three hundred feet of this slowly passing herd of beasts, with the special performance by the two lionesses, and was perfectly delighted. I myself was glad to feel that there had been no need for any shooting to disturb the idyllic peace that reigned.

We remained in that region for several days. A sudden meeting with a savage rhinoceros might have ended badly for us, for only a few yards separated us when I detected the horn among the boughs and cut short the planned attack with a quick shot between the eyes. But our attempt to photograph hippopotami grazing ashore failed. They would never leave their cool element until the light was too poor for taking photographs.

After ten days of wonderful open-air life here, we moved off again over the western edge of the crater towards Serengeti. But it was a tough job to get up to the edge, for the inner wall is fearfully steep, and we had to travel along winding animal tracks. We pitched camp by the river Oldoway, at the time dried up, where we had to dig deep into the sand to find drinking-water. We heard not long afterwards that most remarkable discoveries of fossils had been made just at that spot — a complete skeleton of a man, as well as parts of skeletons of long extinct species of buffalo. Remains of hippopotami and fossilized horns of bushbuck and waterbuck were evidence that once, in the morning of time, the great plains had been forests and lakes.

It was part of our plan of travel to hunt with the movie camera along the western edge of the mountain massif as far as Lake Eyassi, follow the eastern shore of this lake to M'bulu, and at Babati meet our truck, which was to drive us back to the dubious blessings of civilization. It is a fact that we had already thoroughly discussed the bill of fare of our first dinner at Arusha, for men can be thus. Meanwhile Cooper rattled off one roll of film after another — buffalo and rhinoceros at home; elephants, some in herds, others gloomy, meditative recluses, in a hilly landscape clothed with delicious green.

The M'bulu tribe which inhabits these regions are interesting, intelligent people, with fine features, who migrated from the northward a few hundred years ago — Hamites, with a very small admixture of Bantu. They are positively the only blacks with whom I have come into contact who regard theft as the worst of sins, and one never loses anything when traveling through their country. Ordinarily, respect for the rights of property is not of formidable dimensions among African blacks.

I should perhaps add that one meets in this region a fragment of a race dating from the very earliest times, when these parts of Africa were inhabited by bushmen and dwarfs. This tribe — the Digi-digi — is only a few hundred strong, lives in wretched huts, and leads a kind of nomad existence; like the lions on the plain, it moves with the game and lives entirely by hunting. The little people — their average height is a little over four feet — are darker-skinned than their cousins in South Africa and the Congo forest, but otherwise of the same type — nervous, half savage, and desiring only to be allowed to live as their fathers have lived.

Our hunting expedition with camera and rifle was nearing its end. Many wonderful scenes had been impressed upon our memory, and yet the great stage-manager Nature had been pleased to keep the most magnificent till the last — the view from the M'bulu escarpment. In the firm conviction that the human eye could never grow tired of gazing on all this beauty, Cooper and I later settled down there — we each bought a farm in

IN CRATERLAND

the district — and neither of us has regretted having done so.

And so the truck met us. We drove back by bad roads to Arusha — but I shall never forget that journey. It gave me a farm and it gave me a friend, who I know is my friend for always.

X. *Cannibals*

It happened one night up at Isiolo, in northern Kenya. I remember that I had turned in rather early that evening in the hope of getting a really good night's rest. But I had not been asleep in my tent for three hours before I was awakened by a curious rumbling sound. I have heard many animals, but this was something quite new to my ears. It sounded exactly like the buzzing of a motor. Absurd! There were no motor-roads up there! But the mystery must be cleared up; I rolled out of my bed and peeped out through the opening of the tent. Yes, it was a car, driving across country in the middle of the pitch-dark night. There must be a brave and enterprising man at the wheel of that car!

CANNIBALS

His name was Sir Charles Markham. I learned this after we had wakened the boys, had the lights lit and the drinks set out on the table. But to what did I owe the honor of Sir Charles's visit? One is not very particular about visiting-hours in the backwoods of Africa, but all the same . . .

" My business," Sir Charles replied, " is this. I want you to take my wife and me on a safari from the east to the west coast. As the crow flies, you understand, straight. Imagine a ruler . . . "

" But there's no straight road."

" Then we must cut our way through."

I looked at Sir Charles rather more closely. There was no doubt that he was absolutely sober. Was he sitting there and pulling my leg? It did not look as if he was.

What answer was one to give to such a proposal? I began to expound. I pointed out to him, to begin with, that I was surely not the right man, as I had never been on the west coast, and that he could certainly find some more suitable leader in Nairobi. But he would not hear of it at all.

" I've come to you because I want you to do it," he explained. " It's no use your trying to wriggle out of it, because it's no good."

" But have you considered that such a safari would take an inordinately long time? "

"I can give two years, and that ought to be enough," Sir Charles decided.

It was clearly not worth while to make further objections. I guessed that my old friend Sir Robert Coryndon, then Governor of Kenya, had impressed upon Markham that he must not start on his journey without taking me, and it was best to resign myself. After another drink and a short discussion of the economic side of the business — which was arranged easily enough — we started on our journey into the heart of Africa, to the great lakes, the gloomy Congo forests, and the banks of the Nile. But let me do justice to Sir Charles by saying at once that both he and his wife were glad that there were roads, even if they did not lead us straight to our goal.

Many years ago I took part in another safari in the Congo forests. We had got our porters at Mahagi, and as the expedition was to take a considerable time, we had no less than 260 men, all pretty heavily loaded — 60 lb. per man. On the third day a hundred of them bolted; consequently, when we fell in in the morning there were 6,000 lb. of baggage without porters. But one must be prepared for such small mishaps. I sent the other members of the expedition on ahead and waited myself with the things that had been left behind until I could raise fresh porters; and during this mobilization I learned that we had chanced to pitch our camp in Julu's kingdom.

This was no bad news! I knew, from both books and talks, how bravely Julu had fought with Kabba Rega in Samuel Baker's time, and by playing on that string one ought to be able to promote one's own ends. I wrote a letter to his black Majesty in the Mangalla language, couched in diplomatic phraseology, asked him if he would not honor me with a visit, and sent off a messenger with the letter.

Late in the afternoon the old man arrived on horseback. I had had a tent put up for him, prepared a good bed, and ordered a fine dinner. It was with real pleasure that I looked forward to meeting a leading chief of ancient lineage, who would certainly be able to tell me a great deal and clear up many obscure historical questions.

It was as I had guessed — the old fellow succumbed easily to a little attention from a white man, and when I said that I knew his name well, and had heard of his glorious battles with Kabba Rega, he was radiant. I expect he got the idea that the story of his deeds was common property in Europe, and that the reputation he had won with his spear had been enshrined in history.

Nor had I miscalculated in expecting to receive detailed information about certain complications, and their background, during the years of war which preceded the final decision in the interior of Africa.

The bald facts are a matter of history, and scarcely possess the right to exist alongside the personal memories of actual events which I was now hearing. We sat and talked till long after midnight, but before we had finished I took care to drop a hint of my trouble with the porters.

"You sleep well and don't worry," said Julu. "Tomorrow morning I'll get you two hundred porters, and you can choose the hundred best. And I shall tell them to do a double day's march so that you can rejoin your party before sunset."

It sounded splendid. Certainly experience had told me not to rely on African kings, but Julu was not one of those empty talkers, and I knew that there was power behind his words. At dawn he summoned his subordinate chiefs. They sat down in a ring round him at a respectful distance and he gave them his commands in whispers. I did not understand a syllable of what he said, but when he had finished, the mighty men vanished like smoke.

Two hours later the two hundred bearers stood drawn up before me, and they were all sturdy fellows, so that I chose more or less at random. But I have never had such a homogeneous corps of willing and attentive porters; they were with me for a long time.

Their attachment to me probably originated in their ideas of my relationship to their dreaded old chieftain, whose special favorite they supposed me to be.

Six years later I passed through those regions again, but unfortunately did not get an opportunity of visiting the old man and thanking him for his kindness in the past. But Julu, having heard that I was there, sent me a fine goat as a present, an extraordinary attention on his part. Circumstances just then did not allow me to show my gratitude to him, and as I knew that I should be passing through his country again before very long, I left the matter to a future occasion. But it was rash of me. When I came that way for the third time and sought contact with Julu, I heard that he was dead. All that I could do was to consecrate to him a thought full of sorrow and gratitude — sorrow because with him died an era of wild, fantastic adventure, an era in which the names of Livingstone, Stanley, Samuel Baker, and Speke shine like bright stars in the night that before had been so dark.

On the same expedition I came to the Gombari region. I was now in darkest Africa, where cannibalism flourished only a few years ago, and even to-day, without doubt, many a dainty human steak finds its way into the pot.

One evening I visited an old chief in his hut and found him sitting by the fire smoking his long banana-stem pipe. We exchanged the usual greetings, bore witness to our mutual respect, and then settled down to a chat. At last I succeeded in steering the conversation into a channel which just then was of special interest to me.

" Tell me," I said, going straight to the point, " what human flesh tastes like, and how you used to cook it. Which are the titbits? "

He spread out his hands in deprecation. Certainly he had heard talk of such barbarous customs, but that was a thing that belonged to the past. He himself had never tasted human flesh and could not understand how I could have had such an absurd idea.

But I did not drop the subject, and when the old man found that I knew a little more about the matter than he had expected, he became a trifle more communicative. He remembered, too, having heard from my boys that I was no Government official, but only a traveling hunter who had never betrayed any black man's confidence, and he suddenly burst out:

"You're here hunting elephants. When you have shot an elephant you give your servants the meat, but eat chicken and eggs. The same with me! When I had won a fight and taken prisoners I gave my men both the dead and the prisoners, but ate chicken and eggs myself. But," he added with a roguish smile, which furrowed his old face into a thousand wrinkles, "I believe the best part is what one sits on."

Almost everywhere in the interior of the Congo cannibalism was an everyday occurrence as late as the early years of this century.

In these parts the blacks are always short of meat. As there are no pastures, they cannot keep cattle or sheep. Game is scarce and elephants hard to kill, so that it is certainly hunger for meat which has been the main stimulus to cannibalism. In more recent years, of course, everything possible has been done to stop it, and the rising generation has certainly never practiced cannibalism to any extent worth mentioning; but it still happens now and again that a boy disappears on the march and not a trace of him can be found. Doubtless he has found his end in the pot in some remote forest hut.

In the eighties the unhappy prisoners were sold quite openly in the market. As it was not certain that there would be buyers for a whole man, everyone made a chalk mark on the victim to show which part he wanted; and it might be several days before the man was fully subscribed for and sold out. There used to be long discussions and hagglings over the least attractive bits, but not till every single piece had been bought was the victim killed and most carefully dissected, after which the deliveries were made in accordance with the orders placed.

Before I leave the unpleasant subject of cannibalism in Africa I ought, perhaps, to say a few words about the famous Leopard Society, a sect which kills human beings on some kind of religious pretext. For a time this society was an absolute terror to all Central Africa, from the west coast to Ituri, and both the French and Belgian authorities still have the greatest difficulty in keeping it in check.

The members of the society "work" with diabolical skill. It derives its name from the fact that the criminals always try to make it appear that their victim has been killed by a leopard; their skill in covering their tracks is incredible. By means of a stick cut at one end like a leopard's paw they leave the marks of a leopard's paws on the ground, and creep stealthily upon their victims.

I once passed an American mission station in the Gombari district and found the missionary's wife weeping and agitated. The missionary himself was away. Her cook and her house-boy had gone to the river that morning to wash clothes and had there been attacked and captured by cannibals. The cook had managed to escape, but the house-boy had been killed and cut up under the cook's eyes.

A military force which had been sent out arrived rather later. The place pointed out was surrounded; the malefactors were captured and the well-deserved death penalty meted out to them. But nothing was left of the house-boy but his head and a few bones.

XI. *Pygmies*

LET me talk instead of my friends the Wambouti, the dwarf people or pygmies, as they are also called — the ancient inhabitants of forest-clothed Africa, the most primitive people I have ever come across. Intellectually there is no great difference between the Wambouti and the great apes, the chimpanzee and gorilla. I was once talking about them with Selous, the old African expert, and he found it hard to draw a line between the undeveloped South African bushmen and the apes in question. As far as I recollect, the decisive difference he pointed out was that the apes did not understand how to make a fire, but I have hunted in the forests in the interior of the Congo with Wambouti who were completely ignorant of the classic secret that friction

PYGMIES

between hard and soft wood generates enough heat to set light to tinder. And although these people live in regions where it rains every day for two thirds of the year, they have not succeeded in discovering any method of building a hut through whose roof the rain will not come. Moreover, they cannot make themselves the simplest bed; they sleep on two slats laid side by side, and the result is that they get large tumors on their hips.

Once, during my wanderings in the Congo, I had a tame chimpanzee, a pleasant and intelligent beast, which helped me to while away the hours when I was tied to the camp for one reason or another. I had engaged a pygmy to look after my chimpanzee, but I often had the impression that it was the chimpanzee who looked after the man, and not the other way round. A chimpanzee soon learns to untie any knot, so that the way of keeping him tied up is with a lock and chain. I gave his custodian the key of this, but never, during the whole of the time for which I had him, did he find out how to open it. On the contrary, the chimpanzee very soon discovered how the thing worked, and one fine day, when he had got hold of the key in an unguarded moment, he was soon sitting proudly in the nearest tree with the chain wound round his left hand.

The pygmies, now as in the past, earn their livelihood by hunting and fishing, although in latter days they have become, generally speaking, rather dependent economically on surrounding tribes, with whom they carry on trade by barter. Extraordinarily clever and untiring hunters, they are out with their traps, spears, and arrows from morning till night, and they know the habits of the wild beasts better than any professor. By nature they are shy, nervous, and in the highest degree unreliable; for example, it may quite easily happen that a Wambouti who has been engaged as guide will plunge into the forest without the least warning, and let him who can try to find him! The familiar needle in a haystack might be sought with much greater prospect of success. For the Wambouti knows the forest, which he regards as his own, as well as you know the back of your hand.

During my first and fairly long stay among the pygmy people I had as guide and loader a well-made, bearded little Wambouti named Akka. I was then hunting okapi — a very shy and rare beast, as I mentioned earlier — and one of the measures of precaution I took was to let Akka sleep inside the tent door at night. For the enlightenment of those who have any difficulty in seeing the connection, I should say that I was afraid of Akka catching cold and getting a cough if he slept out in the rain at night — okapi-hunting is trying enough anyhow! And not only did he sleep under cover, but I showed him as much kindness in other ways as I could. After six weeks' close companionship and many long conversations — we both spoke Swahili — I asked him how it was that he and the rest of his tribe were still so afraid of white men.

"Why do you run away and hide when we come?" I continued. "You know we don't mean to do you any harm! For example, I don't suppose you yourself are afraid of me any more."

Akka gave me a strange look.

"Afraid!" he repeated. "I'm so afraid of you that if I was not looking after your gun I'd have bolted long ago. I don't dare throw it away. But I am afraid of you — always, all the time."

"But," I objected, "how can you, who are so small and so timid, dare to go right up to an elephant and plunge your short spear into its heart? The elephant is much bigger and much more dangerous than I am!"

Like all Wambouti, Akka was a skillful actor and imitator. The explanation I sought he gave me with a perfect clearness of gesture and mimicry which a European actor might have envied him.

The imaginary elephant raised its massive shape before him. Crouching, with knees bent, he crept nearer, but suddenly started back. The danger of the undertaking had suddenly overwhelmed him. Did not an inevitable and painful death await him?

" But then," Akka continued, in a whisper, " just at that moment I think of my village, how hungry my family are, and how the hunger for meat burns in their eyes. If only I can kill the elephant we shall all have food for many weeks to come. The smell of raw meat tickles my nostrils; I see my beloved, proud of my deed, dancing with the others round the fire that evening, and myself a hero smeared with oil and red ocher. All this drives me on; I take the last two steps with my eyes shut and drive in my spear with all my might right behind the elephant's shoulder."

Out hunting in the Congo forest with little Akka, I once came upon a particularly fine elephant spoor. Local hunters had warned me before of a certain unusually large elephant spoor, whose owner followed tracks that seemed to coincide with these.

" Avoid that spoor," they had said, " for that elephant hasn't a sign of tusks and is very fierce into the bargain."

Anyhow, I measured the spoor, which was an

absolute record — twenty-five and a half inches across! The temptation was too strong; although I had a feeling that the elephant was just the one against which I had been warned, we took up the pursuit. In a few hours we heard the well-known noise of branches being broken down in the forest — our giant elephant was feeding. With noiseless steps we crept nearer inch by inch, and suddenly I caught sight of him in a clearing — yes, that was he. Not tusks enough for a billiard-ball.

We had now to retire as noiselessly as we had come, but the attempt was not successful; we had only gone some ten steps when I was guilty of some unnecessary rustling; the elephant heard us and came rushing at us like a locomotive. I jumped to one side, but Akka ran straight ahead with the elephant hard at his heels. It seemed to be only a matter of seconds before he would be crushed under the elephant's huge feet; the animal had already lifted its trunk to seize him when Akka, as though in self-protection, held up his bow and arrows. Then an astonishing thing happened — the elephant grasped them instead of the man.

When I was to part from Akka, who owned not a thing in the whole world, not even his spear — this belonged to the chief of a neighboring tribe — I said to him:

"I want to give you a present. Is there anything you would particularly like to have?"

Akka meditated a long time, and his puzzled face showed plainly that this meditation cost him a great effort. At last he pointed to the leather belt I wore round my waist, a perfectly ordinary, cheap, everyday belt.

"I'd like to have that," he said.

I could not quite understand what he, who went about stark naked, would do with my belt, but of course! — by all means, here it is.

"But," I said, "that can't be your greatest wish. You can have a lot more than that, you understand. Just say the word."

But little Akka did not understand. He could not think of anything else. His list of desiderata began and ended with the belt. To help him out, I laid before him a blanket, a few sheath-knives, an ax, some pots, and a bit of everything of which I imagined that he and his family could make use — plus a little bag of small coins.

"Can't you use any of all these things, Akka?" I asked.

"Yes," he answered, hesitatingly and timidly, "but I can't have any of them."

"They're yours already, Akka. The whole lot

is yours. Every single thing is yours, and you can do just what you like with it."

Akka's worried, almost despairing expression was irresistible, and I could well understand my other servants when they burst into a roar of laughter. But the right of possession was to Akka something so new, incomprehensible, and alarming that I think it would have been a great relief to him if I had taken everything back — and I shall never forget his face when, after we had said good-by, he put the box in which I had packed his belongings on his head and disappeared into the forest.

The spirit behind the deed, when the pygmy thrusts his spear into the elephant behind the shoulder, is something more than desperate terror. But do not let us exaggerate — the World War afforded many examples of that kind of heroism. But the pygmy people's fear has many gradations and is typical in its way of a certain side of the tribe's mentality. Once, on Cooper's safari, we had before us forest country unknown to our own blacks and could not possibly get hold of any guide who knew the district; but one of the natives in the village where we had pitched camp declared that he could show us the way to a Wambouti village, which lay in the forest only a few days' march away.

"There," said the man, "you can easily get a Wambouti who can show you the way everywhere. If only the whole lot don't bolt into the forest before you get there."

That was the rub! As if I was not aware of our little friends' peculiarities! And to be on the safe side, I sent a couple of natives on ahead to the Wambouti village, six whole hours before we reckoned that we should arrive, with instructions to prepare the pygmies for our visit and make it clear to them that we came with the friendliest intentions, prepared to pay royally for the services they could do us.

But not even this tactical maneuver availed us. Long before our two black emissaries had reached the scene of their diplomatic mission, the pygmies, with their almost supernatural intuition, had scented the approaching danger and fled into the forest. When they arrived the whole village was an empty shell — as it seemed. The boys searched in every hole and corner and were on the point of admitting failure when they heard a whimpering from one of the miserable huts. It appeared that one of the pygmy women, in her hurried departure, had forgotten her child, which had evidently been asleep, but had now suddenly awakened and begun to cry for food.

When mamma came back to fetch the child she was naturally caught at once by my men, and when she had calmed down a little and understood what was afoot, she declared herself ready to help us to get the guide we wanted.

For safety's sake they put a rope round her neck — as I have said, one can never rely on a Wambouti, male or female — and so she had to guide us to the place where the villagers had hidden themselves.

Not a soul! The pygmies might have been swallowed up by the earth. With the knowledge of the Wambouti's habits which I had succeeded in acquiring, I was not particularly surprised, but I knew they must be quite close by. I therefore made one of our natives go about in the forest calling out what our business was. But for all our promises and assurances, and although the husband of the woman and father of the child without the least doubt both heard and saw us from his hiding-place, we shouted in vain!

But when it came to the test, the woman did the job for us. She proved to know the forest well, and after two days' walk she led us by winding tracks to our goal. Then, delighted with a pretty liberal *douceur,* she was allowed to return to her poltroon of a husband and all the other poltroons.

To complete what I have said of the physical appearance and characteristics of the pygmy people, I may mention that their color is much lighter than that of the surrounding tribes, and that their faces beat all records for ugliness, with large mouths and flat noses; I have never seen uglier women. But if nature has been niggardly towards them as regards height, she has been correspondingly generous as regards their bellies, the size of which is sometimes grotesque. But no tailor need apply the measuring tape, for all the clothing the pygmy people require they take from the nearest banana tree — a few leaves behind and in front in a cord round the waist is all that is needed; not even on festal occasions do they trouble to smarten themselves up. And festal occasions are frequent, for the Wambouti love dance and song. I have never seen anything at once so touching and so comic as these little men and women, with their enormous buttocks, tripping round in rhythmic time, their heads swaying from left to right, and interpolating little jumps in the air and pirouettes.

At the same time they are extraordinarily active. They climb trees with the swiftness of monkeys and can swing themselves from tree-top to tree-top, as monkeys do, as quickly as we can move along the ground, or more quickly. But their most conspicuous quality, overshadowing all else, is their ability as trackers. From childhood up, their eyes are accustomed to observe the smallest signs and to draw lightning conclusions from these observations. Where the white man's eyes see nothing but everyday trifles, the Wambouti reads as in an open book of dramatic action and tragic events. A bent grass, a fallen leaf, a mark on a tree-trunk — from these things he constructs a chain of events with a swiftness and an unfailing certainty which no detective in the world can imitate.

Tracking-ability is, of course, an individual quality, and in the Wambouti tribe, as elsewhere, it is more or less pronounced in different individuals, but no pygmy is altogether without it. They all creep forward absolutely noiselessly through the thickest brushwood, and among rustling leaves they move so that the most acute ear cannot hear the slightest sound. It is almost magical. All their movements are so calculated as not to alarm even a wild creature on its guard.

Trackers belonging to other tribes recognize absolutely, without professional jealousy, the superiority of the Wambouti. I once took a Vandoro man named Simba — the best tracker I have met in East Africa — down to the pygmies' country, and we hunted there together for a month. Simba was filled with an expert's delight at the little people's skill, and to me it is always a pleasure to see how these hunters follow game. It is the same pleasure which a fowler at home in Sweden feels when watching a dog at work out in the country — interest coupled with admiration; indeed, enthusiasm.

In the exercise of his art — for an art it is — the tracker's qualities are tested to the uttermost. His patience must know no bounds, his physical endurance must almost exceed a Marathon runner's, and his powers of observation must be keener than Sherlock Holmes's. These qualities enable him to say in the morning where the lion killed his prey last night, where the elephant lay down to rest during the darkest hours, where and between what animals nocturnal love duels to the death were fought out, when the wild beasts went to their waterholes, and where these are situated.

Sight is the only one of the five senses which the native uses in tracking. We white men are also helped by our sense of smell — the buffalo and the elephant and, above all, the waterbuck, have a very strong and peculiar smell — but the blacks have lost this sense, undeniably of considerable value, through their gross abuse of nicotine. Tobacco

WAMBOUTI INFANTRY IN THE FIRING LINE

LIFE HAS LEFT ITS MARKS

plays a large part in the black man's life, and as he snuffs, chews, and smokes from early morning till late at night, it is not surprising that he has injured his sense of smell.

The native grows his own tobacco, dries the leaves, and grinds them in a mortar with a round stone. The Congo Negro does not even wait till the tobacco has dried, but takes it while still green, holds the leaves over the fire for a moment till they are carbonized, and rubs them to powder in his hands. He stuffs them into a little clay head, whose short shaft is thrust into the thick end of a banana-leaf stem, about six feet long. He has previously bored a channel up the stem with a splinter of cane. He gets in this way a very strong and potent pipe of tobacco. One single puff of the cold smoke into the lungs makes him dizzy at once, if he does not become completely unconscious. He does in a little while in any case — and then he has achieved his object.

But those of more cultivated tastes are not content with nicotine. In spite of severe legislation in the different states prohibiting hemp-smoking, this vice is vigorously practiced by the blacks all over Africa. But woe to him who becomes a slave of this habit! The same terrible fate awaits him as the victims of the cocaine vice in Europe.

XII. *Beliefs and Superstitions*

I DO not know why it is, but wherever one goes among hunters — all over the world — one finds the superstitious trait; and you can be sure that Africa is no exception to the rule. The black hunters regard it as a particularly good omen if they meet a snake when they are going out hunting. And there is no question that their superstition is infectious — what other explanation is there for the fact that my own confidence rises several degrees if I come upon a reptile? If sport has been bad until then, luck will turn, and it always does.

Once, on the Nile, I was hunting an old elephant

which had mocked at all my efforts for nearly a month. When we were setting out one morning, we met a black lugging a large python which he had killed. My gun-bearer, old Juma, gave a howl of delight when he saw the snake.

"Now we'll soon get the elephant!" he cried.

The same day two more men appeared, each with a python, and when I myself shot a snake of the same kind the day after, there was no doubt that the old elephant's fate was sealed. In the afternoon I came upon the fresh spoor of eight bull elephants. We took up the pursuit at once, and towards evening we found them all at a river, where they were refreshing themselves by bathing and squirting water.

All the same, I was rather disappointed — the old beast with the large tusks whom I was after was not among them, and none of the others had any tusks worth mentioning. Suddenly Juma plucked at my coat and pointed — there, not ten steps away, stood the giant I had so long been searching for! He fell stone dead at my first bullet. The python's doing, of course!

Carl Lagercrantz recalls a similar episode in his book about Africa. On the way out to our hunting-ground I drove over a black mamba.

"Now we shall see lions," I remarked.

Lagercrantz looked at me and laughed. But it is a fact that he killed his first two lions that afternoon.

The hunting-grounds of Africa swarm with snakes — of all kinds and all degrees of poisonousness — but it is comparatively seldom that one sees them. They are shy creatures, which seek refuge in holes and nooks before one can catch sight of them. The puff adder is the sole exception. It likes to lie asleep in the sun and is often too lazy to wriggle away, even if it notices the approaching danger. If one treads on it, death is not far off, but if the white hunter is wise he will always make the black guide walk a few yards in front of him; his sharp eyes seldom miss a puff adder.

Talking of superstition, the pygmy people are a very fertile soil for everything in that line. I will content myself with quoting a single example. The men carry round their necks a wooden whistle on a strap of dried squirrel skin, and this is used to whistle away rain as soon as a threatening black cloud rises in the sky. The moment a shower threatens, an ear-splitting whistling breaks out in the Wambouti village. Nine times out of ten, of course, the rain comes on, but the tenth time it may happen that the clouds pass by without discharging any water-floods, and then the pygmy is firmly convinced that it is his whistle that has done the trick. He believes in it as in a god and would never go out into the forest without having his protection against rain with him.

The blacks' superstition goes hand in hand with their deceitfulness. I was once out elephant-hunting with a Swede, Lalle Ekman, and Ekman succeeded in bringing down a beast with particularly fine tusks. But it was rather late in the day, so we decided to leave the cutting up and the removal of the tusks till next morning. To be able to find the place where the elephant lay without any great difficulty, Ekman — following a classical example — marked the route home with leaves torn from the trees.

But when, next morning, we set out to take possession of Ekman's valuable property we found that the trail we had laid had disappeared. The black scoundrels had taken care to clear away every single leaf during the night, so as to make it impossible for us to find the place, or at least delay our finding it. In the latter object they succeeded admirably; we did not find the spot for two days, and then nothing was left of Ekman's elephant but a few bones; all the rest, tusks and flesh, was stolen. Our own attempts to secure justice having failed, of course we reported the theft to the authorities, and the thieves were soon arrested. Ekman got his tusks, and the rascals their punishment.

One day I shot an elephant not far from Akka's village, and soon the whole tribe was there, women with babies, old and young, I should think about fifty all told. It was almost incredible how quickly a gigantic beast like an elephant can be cut up into small pieces by a crowd of hungry natives. The men carve without any system whatever. They are like hyenas flinging themselves on a fallen animal. The women stand behind their husbands and receive the pieces of meat which are flung to them. Others make baskets of lianas and big leaves; places are arranged for the smoking of the flesh; they all sleep round their fires at night, and the meat is roasted and smoked for three days. The stench is fearful. Shouting and singing, fighting and dancing turn the place into a fair-ground. When the meat has been well smoked, it keeps for several months even in that tropical heat, and the children fill themselves with meat till their stomachs are like balloons.

I have tried to describe the reaction of a normal human mind when confronted with buffalo, elephant, and lion. The buffalo's mass affair is a furious outburst of elemental violence; the elephant inspires fear by its enormous strength, its cunning, and its gigantic size; and a wounded lion tries the nerves of the hunter who knows with what astonishing swiftness it attacks. But I conceived an even greater respect for the gorilla when I had found out the difficulties which the hunting of that animal involved.

I had gone to Kribi, in what was formerly the German Cameroons, on behalf of the Philadelphia Museum. The expedition was equipped by George Vanderbilt, and its task was to supply the museum with a few particularly representative specimens of the gorilla and pygmy elephant. It was the first time I had come into contact with these giant African apes.

To be on the safe side I had engaged both Juma and Simba, two of the most skillful trackers in Africa, whom I have already mentioned. The country in which we had to hunt for the gorillas was some of the worst I have seen — such impenetrably thick growth that the enterprise seemed all but hopeless, though I think I can say I am not one of those who give up an attempt when hardly begun. Juma had persuaded me to take off both boots and clothes to avoid unnecessary noise, and day after day, often crawling on all fours, we pursued a giant gorilla; but, although it was only a few yards away from us all the time, it never let us see enough of its black body for it to be worth while to fire. After ten days' unsuccessful hunting I had to enlist the help of natives in order to get the specimens the museum desired; two giants were secured, and two younger males.

But the pygmy elephants we shot ourselves, a full-grown bull and a cow which had calved the year before. The most peculiar characteristic of these little-known animals is that the soles of their feet are almost smooth, while those of their larger relations are as rough as the tread of a motor-car tire to prevent the creature from slipping. But the elephant is classified partly by the shape of its ears, partly by the number of nails on its feet, and men of science hold that there are six different species between the west and east coasts.

I have also been out several times with Alfred Vanderbilt. The first time we went elephant-hunting in the country round Voi, but it was a miserable business. We had had a sight of a big elephant which defied us for two and a half months. We were continually in harness all this time, wore out many pairs of boots, smashed up an aeroplane and three cars, but all to no purpose. We did not see even the tip of the elephant's tail. Vanderbilt was a thoroughly good fellow, but none the less I expected dismissal from day to day. I have no doubt that he saw the honest endeavors I was making, but he must have thought that he might be able to get hold of a luckier safari leader.

One afternoon we were sitting chatting as usual when Vanderbilt suddenly grew absent and thoughtful. "Now it's coming," I thought. "All right! I'll bear my fate like a man!"

"Look here, Bror," he began, "suppose I come back next year! What do you think is the longest time I can have to spend to get a big elephant?"

I answered shamefacedly that two months ought to be enough.

"Let's say three months, to be on the safe side," said Vanderbilt nodding. "And you can be sure that I'll come. This is the first time I've been after anything that money can't buy, and these two and a half months have been the best fun I've ever had."

Not long afterwards I was hunting in those very parts with Captain Frederick Guest[1] and his daughter, and we shot in a week's hunting four bull elephants with tusks weighing on an average 116 lb. The goddess of sport is certainly capricious.

[1] Captain the Honorable Frederick E. Guest, died 1937.

Here at Voi lives my tracker Simba, a fellow with good eyes and a hunter of outstanding skill. He belongs to a very small native tribe, which has lived by hunting for generations. They have smuggled hundreds of tons of ivory to the coast and sold them to the Arabs. Their sole weapon is a simple bow, which they often manage with greater success than we handle the best weapons that modern gunsmiths can produce.

Simba once showed me a bow which he had had for many years and with which he said he had killed no less than eighty elephants. Of course the main reason for killing the beasts is a mercenary one, but the love of hunting and the desire for adventure certainly play their part. By the campfire Simba often turned the conversation to these hunts, to which the strictly administered game laws have now put a stop. He narrated how he had often escaped dying of thirst only by killing an elephant in time and drinking the water which it carries in a specially constructed vessel in its stomach. He told me how he had seen his best friend and hunting comrade killed and trampled into a wet stain on the earth under the feet of a furious elephant. He revealed to me how he had been hunted for days on end by the Government police, who had got wind of the lucrative trade. He described how he had con-

BELIEFS AND SUPERSTITIONS

ducted his caravans to the coast by night to sell the tusks his good luck as a hunter had brought him. And he did not conceal his shame when he told how he had once been captured and got two years' hard labor for his illegal hunting.

Now he has his home near Voi. The ivory has brought him cattle, and three wives till his durra field. Like his temporary employer, he is very fond of beer; mead is brewed in big casks in his secluded village, and when we hunt in these parts a calabash of fresh-brewed beer often comes to Simba's table. He has been all over Africa with me twice. He has ridden on camel-back along Lake Chad, he has motored to Timbuktu, and gone by boat the whole way round the Cape from Dakar to Mombasa. He has seen the richest parts of inland Africa, where the soil is perhaps more fertile than anywhere else on earth, but for him the monotonous thorny scrubland by the sandy river Voi is the most glorious place in the world — home! This is the confession of a simple black man, but it springs from just the same feelings with which we Swedes return to our bare north, our hearts beating with joy and gratitude, after we have seen the tropics' gorgeous sights and their fantastic, wasteful luxuriance.

XIII. *"I'm the Prince of Wales"*

ON November 16, 1928 the Prince of Wales was to come to Arusha on his way from Nairobi to Dar-es-Salaam. It was an unofficial visit, but all the same the town was making a holiday of it; all the neighboring farmers were to come; the hotel was giving a dance; the Masai had arranged a great *ngoma*. A battalion of the King's African Rifles was paraded for inspection; a football match had been fixed up; in short, there was as complete a festival atmosphere as the little town at the foot of Meru could achieve.

My wife and I had driven our 115 miles into the town like the rest and pitched camp not far from the hotel. I was just shaking a cocktail when a little man came into the tent and said:

"I'M THE PRINCE OF WALES"

"I'm the Prince of Wales and should like to make your acquaintance."

"You could not have chosen a more suitable moment," I replied with a smile, and put the ice-cold shaker on the table.

We drank to each other and sat down. The Prince asked if I could accompany him for a few days and help him to bag a lion. Of course I willingly placed myself at his disposal and began my duties with him that very evening in the most pleasant way imaginable — my wife and I were invited to dinner at his hotel. It was a rather informal little party, which ended with dancing, and while the others were dancing I had an opportunity of discussing and planning the lion-hunt of the next two days with my old friend Finch-Hatton,[1] who was already a member of the Prince's hunting party. Unfortunately the Prince had not more than two days to spare — no one knew then that he could extend his time — so we had to look for lion in the immediate neighborhood. Finch-Hatton and I therefore decided to pitch camp at the foot of Mount Ufiomi — not far from my farm, by the way.

At half past seven next morning the hunting

[1] The Honorable D. G. Finch-Hatton, brother to the present Earl of Winchilsea, killed while flying in East Africa, May 1931.

party left Arusha in a slight drizzle. It was a regular cavalcade of cars; I drove with Finch-Hatton in his Hudson, but only for a few miles. We hit a rock, which excellently suited the rest of the party, who were longing for tea. Now we had a good excuse for stopping and making tea while the car was being repaired. The tea-making went well, but the repairs were not at all successful — the Hudson's gasoline-tank was so badly cracked that it could not be patched up, and one of the trucks had to take the cripple in tow. Then both the weather and the road grew better as we approached Babati, which we reached just in time for lunch.

Here Captain Moore, game ranger at Arusha, met us with recent reports of both buffalo and rhinoceros, but what did we want with buffalo and rhinoceros when we were after lion? The Prince agreed with me, and I thereupon drove off to reconnoiter the ground and put down my kills.

But on the first day we had no luck. I had set my bait near the village of Kwakuchinjas, and the lion had been there and had a feed all right, but when the royal party came, the ungrateful brute had cleared off. We had to return to Babati with long faces, though the most crestfallen of the party was naturally myself.

"I'M THE PRINCE OF WALES"

I was not merely crestfallen, however — I was angry, and swore that the Prince should have his lion. And so he did. It happened like this.

I had put down the kills by night, after shooting several zebras, and when I visited them at dawn I found two lions on no less than four of the shot beasts — eight lions in all. I waited till they had finished their morning meal without disturbing them, but when they had withdrawn into the shade of the brushwood for their day's rest, I sent for the royal party.

Unfortunately the boys I had sent for to take part in a drive had not turned up, so when I had placed the Prince and Finch-Hatton at the most likely spot for the first lions, I had to constitute myself beater along with a few drivers and the Prince's suite. The lions broke out, but not till we had a few exciting moments when one of them rushed out, roaring savagely, only a few yards from the Prince's adjutant, who was armed only with a shotgun.

At the next kill things went better, although the ground was not so favorable. I myself do not like hunting lion in long grass, and it was only after much hesitation that Finch-Hatton and I decided to try it. But I proposed that the Prince should have more than one gun with him; and Finch-

AFRICAN HUNTER

Hatton, Captain Moore, and the Prince's two equerries were placed on one side of the copse into which the lions had withdrawn to rest.

For a description of what followed I will take the liberty of quoting the Prince of Wales himself. His diary of experiences in Africa, which his secretary turned into a book,[2] contains the following passage:

" Similar tactics were employed with this difference; that Blixen (whose attitude towards lions is that of the prophet Daniel) decided to be the sole beater. He had not gone far when a lion appeared at the edge of the covert. It turned rapidly and re-entered the bush. ' Shoo,' said Blixen, not to be denied, ' Shoo,' and he clapped his hands. Out bounded the lion.

" He really looked rather fine. Broadside on, he galloped across the front. H.R.H. was shooting with a 350 double-barrel Express lent to him by Grigg. With the first barrel he missed cleanly and cleverly. A little rattled at that, he took more time to his second shot. The left-hand barrel was fired at the lion when he was 140 yards away. The grass was tallish, and the big, yellow beast went bounding through it in great leaps. It was a difficult shot because of the grass, and a long one. But it was a

[2] *Sport and Travel in East Africa,* by Patrick R. Chalmers; quoted by courtesy of the publishers, E. P. Dutton & Co.

HIPPOS AT PLAY

Photo, Viscountess

RIPON FALLS, THE SOURCE OF THE VICTORIA NIL
AS IT COMES OUT OF LAKE VICTORIA

"I'M THE PRINCE OF WALES"

lucky one also, for it knocked the lion over and over. H.R.H. reloaded and ran up to where it lay.

"The lion lay still after the shot, but on closer approach he got on to his legs and made off, but he was unable to get very far. He then stopped and wheeling round, obviously intended to charge. By this time H.R.H. was close up to him and before he could get going gave him both barrels again, hitting him full in the chest each time. The last shot dropped him anew, but the grass was so long it was not until the rifle was right on top of him that he was seen to be dead.

"The beast was an old one, in good condition, and measured 104 inches as he lay. The 'boys' set to work to skin it forthwith, while every one else sat down to lunch, all very happy with themselves, especially Blixen."

Thus far the Prince's notes.

Next day's buffalo-hunting yielded no buffalo, but a whole day of wearisome clambering over difficult ground, and this should, according to program, have been the end of the royal hunting in those parts, as the following day was set apart for a visit to Dodoma. But in the evening the Prince asked me if I thought there would be a chance of a few more days' good hunting if he could come back when his official duties were over.

"Certainly, Your Royal Highness," I replied;

"if I can only have full powers to requisition the native help I think we need, the thing is done."

The full powers I sought were given me at once, and next day I went to the local Government official.

"I want three hundred fighting men for the Prince," I explained, "plus their chief."

"Why not five hundred?" he asked, smiling.

"Why not? Let me have five hundred, then."

And next day I had them — five hundred tall M'bulu warriors, armed with spears and with a loincloth for uniform, fearless warriors of one of the best tribes in Africa, under the command of my old friend the chief Michaeli.

The camp was moved to my farm, and the same evening I held a council of war with Michaeli. We plotted and planned both long and well, and before we had finished, every buffalo and rhinoceros in the whole district was, in theory, tracked down and reserved for the Prince.

The country where the hunt was to take place is mountainous and wooded, with open fields and plains here and there. The left wall of the Rift valley rises to a height of twelve hundred feet above the valley. There are no roads; all hunting has to be done on foot.

At the appointed time — two p.m. — the Prince

"I'M THE PRINCE OF WALES"

came back after two days' exhausting official duties. We had a light lunch and went off at once to a place three hundred yards farther down the valley. We saw buffaloes, but had no chance of getting in a shot.

I must mention here an incident which illustrates the natives' mentality and their loyalty to their own chiefs. Finch-Hatton and I were sitting on a rock with the Prince, resting, while the five hundred warriors were sitting round us waiting for their chief, who had gone off to get information about some other buffaloes. I saw him approaching and said to the Prince that he should notice the discipline which the blacks observe in dealing with their chief. Michaeli was wearing only their simple everyday garb, but when he came near, all the warriors rose with their spears, then laid the spears on the ground and stood upright at attention. It is not good manners to meet one's chief with a weapon in one's hand.

We hunted all that day and did not come home till long after dark. It was a tiring hunt in long grass among high mountains. Several of the farmers and Government officials living in the neighborhood had been invited to dinner, and although the Prince of Wales had that day received the first telegrams telling him of his father's illness, he entertained his guests till nearly midnight. He and I sat up talking for an hour or two, but directly we parted I heard the notes of an accordion from the little tent in which the Prince lived alone. I well understood his mood — he had spoken of one thing and another pretty openly earlier that night — and now he was trying to drive away his anxiety and fear with a little music. I went in to him and we continued our interrupted conversation for a little while, but at last I could not keep my eyes open any longer and had to say good-night for the second time. And the last thing I heard before I fell asleep was the melancholy minor tones of the Prince's accordion.

I relate this episode only to show what immense endurance and sportsmanlike spirit this man possesses. That same day he had driven nearly 180 miles in a car over rough roads, had hunted for six hours, and had then for a whole evening entertained and chatted with a dozen people whom he had never seen before and would probably never see again — while he was consumed with anxiety and fear on account of the illness of a beloved father, the issue of which might have for himself consequences of the deepest significance.

Next morning we photographed one or two rhinoceroses and went for a drive in the country

"I'M THE PRINCE OF WALES"

round. It had been arranged that we should have lunch afterwards in my simple cottage, which we did. After lunch the Prince took me aside, and I shall never forget the tone of his voice when he said:

"I say, Blixen, you really oughtn't to let your wife live in a tumbledown place like this."

I naturally felt ashamed — though my wife had never complained — and inwardly promised to put things right. Then the camera hunt was resumed, without any particular experiences which are worth printing.

On Tuesday, November 27 — I quote from the book on the Prince of Wales's hunting expeditions in Africa — the party left the camp for Dodoma. On the way a short visit was paid to Kondoa, where a telegram awaited the Prince. It was from London, but in a cipher which neither he nor anyone else could read. Anxious and worried, the Prince put on full speed ahead for Dodoma, for not till he got there could he get the telegram deciphered. Not that it was really necessary; for at Dodoma were telegrams from the Prime Minister, from Admiral Halsey, and from Sir Godfrey Thomas. The news from Buckingham Palace was alarming, and the cautious wording of the messages made them seem more alarming still. The Prince had to return to London at once. His hunting expedition was over. And at any moment he might have to open a blue and white envelope informing him that he was no longer Prince of Wales.

He left Dodoma at four in the morning of November 28 by the Governor's train, but he had to wait three days for a cruiser which was to take him to Europe. The ship entrusted with the task was the *Enterprise*, the same vessel which not so long ago conveyed the luckless Emperor of Abyssinia from Djibouti to Haifa. The Prince described this journey to me later as one of the most awful experiences he had ever had.

But before we parted he asked me if I thought there was anyone who had specially deserved a present of some kind. I answered that I thought the chief Michaeli, who had on several occasions showed his goodwill, would certainly be very grateful for a little memento, a knife or something else of that kind. A month or two after the Prince had reached home something much finer arrived — "the King's Medal for Africans," a beautiful medal to be worn round the neck on a silver chain, the highest distinction a colored man can receive. I have never seen a happier man than Michaeli was then.

XIV. "One of the Toughest Sportsmen"

IN January 1930 the Prince resumed his hunting expedition in Africa which the illness of the King of England had brought to such a sorry end. This time he did Africa thoroughly, starting from Cape Town. The steamer *Modasa* brought His Royal Highness from Zanzibar to Tanga and Mombasa, where he arrived on the morning of February 11. Finch-Hatton, who had been warned by the Governor, Sir Edward Grigg, was waiting for the Prince at Government House, and so was lunch. One may be sure that sport was talked in the dining-room at and after lunch.

But there was not only talking — decisions were

taken also. The Prince decided, at the suggestion of his advisers, to devote ten days to hunting in the region southwest of Kilimanjaro. He was to start the same evening in a special train to be provided by the Government, and travel to Maungu. I was to meet him there, and we hunters would proceed by car to Mount Kasigau and look for elephant. If Kasigau fell short of our expectations, we could go on by train to Maktau and, starting from there, hunt over the country in the neighborhood of Jipi and the Paré mountains.

It proved to be Jipi. At Kasigau we certainly found an elephant spoor, which we followed pretty well from sunrise to sunset and on which each of us wore out our boots, but we never saw an elephant; and so we returned to the car and later to the train, which conveyed us to our second choice. We three — the Prince, Finch-Hatton, and I — started out early the next morning, February 14, with a few black porters.

Finch-Hatton had sent some native scouts on in advance, and we had not walked far before the fellows appeared and informed us, in a state of considerable excitement, that they had seen an elephant quite close by, a real big fellow with enormous tusks. His spoor was there too, all right, and it was not hard to see that it was fresh. The

"ONE OF THE TOUGHEST SPORTSMEN"

size of the spoor was really impressive. According to the Prince's notes it was then 9.45 a.m.

Then began what is called a forced march. I am afraid that the Prince, excited by the thought of a record bag, began rather too violently. We covered over ten miles, in a difficult country and fearful heat, in little more than two hours — good going indeed! My experience of elephants' habits told me that the beast would probably take a little siesta during the hottest hours — and we thought we could do the same. Moreover, there is no pleasure in lunching at a jogtrot, and our stomachs were crying for food; so we looked for a shady spot and allowed ourselves an hour's rest.

But perhaps we ought not to have done so. The elephant had evidently been in a hurry to get to the Paré mountains and had fed as he went; his spoor was still plain, but nothing indicated that he had rested anywhere. His gigantic spoor went southwest almost as straight as a ruler.

Our forced march continued hour after hour. I could not help looking at the Prince from time to time out of the corner of my eye. Finch-Hatton and I, of course, were trained cross-country runners, and I knew by experience that H.R.H. had remarkable powers of physical endurance, but he had had no opportunity of training himself in this particular kind of walking. Nothing in his expression showed that he was tired, that the blisters on his feet burned like fire — he did not give a sign of feeling inclined to call a halt. It was the darkness that stopped us.

We had to pitch our tents on the open plain, without even a bush in sight. The Prince's comfortless little Boy Scout tent was up in three minutes, while Finch-Hatton and I slept on the bare ground. There was nothing to prevent the Prince from surrounding himself with all possible luxury and comfort, but he is notoriously not that sort of man. Despising all effeminate softness in others, he makes the greatest demands on himself. I can assert without hesitation that he is one of the three or four toughest sportsmen I have been out with, perhaps the toughest of them all.

We did not get many hours' sleep that night — we set off again before daybreak. The first rays of the sun lit up the spoor of the giant elephant; it looked fresher than on the previous day, which of course spurred us to further efforts. But as the sun rose higher it increased our difficulties; the volcanic soil burned under our feet; there was no merciful shade within reach; every step caused us horrible pain. But on we went.

Just before sunset that day we had pursued the

elephant over forty miles; the spoor positively smelt of him, but we had not seen him. Our feet were in a deplorable state, but give up? Not we! We should get the old fellow next day.

But next day was like the one before — except that our feet almost refused to do service. Our pace had to be reduced, but not only on account of our feet — our provisions began to run short; we had to content ourselves with half rations, and that, too, reduced our strength. Still we did not give up, but dragged ourselves along after the spoor as quickly as we could.

But on the morning of the fourth day it did not look as if any of us three would be able to put on his boots. A specialist in sore feet, water-blisters, and skin complaints would have had his fill for a long time to come. But on went our boots, anyhow, up we got, and on we toiled.

About two o'clock in the afternoon the spoor — which looked as if it had been made only a few minutes earlier — turned off in the direction of a fairly dense wood. Suddenly Finch-Hatton became aware of the elephant, crept forward quite noiselessly, and was able to establish that it was the beast we were looking for, as big as a house and with tusks which must weigh nearly four hundred pounds. As silently as a spirit he worked his way closer. The vegetation was, as I have said, very dense; the Prince of Wales had to use a peephole to get anything like a clear field of fire, and just then the disaster happened. Some cursed dry twig had taken care to place itself under the Prince's foot; the twig snapped, the elephant listened for a quarter of a second with ears spread wide, and then there was a crashing among the bushes — the beast set off at full speed at a rate of forty miles an hour and was gone before we could count three.

To assert that we flung ourselves down on the ground for a professional discussion of our mistakes and errors would perhaps be a slight exaggeration. We sat down where we stood, and not much was said, but the words uttered were sincere and vigorous.

Back at Nairobi, assembled in the Governor's palace for a fresh council of war. We had to work out plans for the Prince's next safari, taking into consideration that he had to be in Khartoum on April 13, I think, at the latest, and so it was decided that he should spend the next three weeks camera hunting with the Masai.

We set off at once. We drove by car to Kajiado, where Clarence Buxton joined the party; and at the camp at Selangi, Captain Ritchie, the game

"ONE OF THE TOUGHEST SPORTSMEN"

warden of the district, attached himself to us. He was full of good news — fifteen lions had, practically speaking, caught him by the slack of his pants; there were rhinoceros and elephant quite close by. The camera, therefore, need not remain inactive, but it was no use casting an eye on one's rifle, for here we were in a part of the southern game preserve. Unfortunately the weather at first was useless for all photography — the drizzle was hopeless. But next day it had cleared up. Sunshine, the best visibility imaginable, without the least haze — ideal photographing weather.

First the Prince got an elephant. Sanctuary or no, one had to have one's rifle ready all the time to protect the photographers, for one is entitled to kill an attacking beast in all circumstances. A human life is worth more than an animal's — that principle is recognized without reservation. But the Prince's elephant showed no signs of ill humor. On the contrary, he stood still and twitched his big ulster-like ears, rumbled placidly, and when the process was finished uttered a short trumpet note — it sounded almost like "Thanks!"

The rhinoceros which was number two on the program was harder to deal with. The mastodon was lying asleep in the sunshine; so he had to be got on to his legs as a preliminary, and Captain

Ritchie undertook to play the part of alarm clock. The rhinoceros was devilish. The sound of the alarm was not to his taste; like many two-legged beings, he wanted to go on sleeping, and when he was not allowed to do so he became soured and angry. He glowered at the Prince's camera. So it was that thing that had disturbed his pleasant morning slumber! If that was so, he would see that it was the last time.

The living tank rolled forward to the assault on the Prince, who went on quietly clicking his roll of film. The rhinoceros grew swiftly on the picture, which was just what was wanted. Ritchie fired a warning shot in the hope that the beast would see reason and alter its course. But it did not, and now the raging beast must definitely be stopped, for no one may approach the heir to the English throne in such cavalier fashion, however democratic in his general disposition the latter may be. The shots from Finch-Hatton's and Ritchie's rifles rang out simultaneously when the rhinoceros was hardly six feet from the Prince, who never moved. But the animal fell as heavy and lifeless as only a sack weighing a few tons can fall.

In their capacity of nomad shepherds the Masai have certain privileges. Among other things, they are allowed to reduce the number of lions even

"ONE OF THE TOUGHEST SPORTSMEN"

within the preserves as a measure of protection for their cattle. From time immemorial the Masai's religion has strictly forbidden them to eat the flesh of game; a breach of the law, according to their belief, would mean some immediate disaster to their cattle. Game, accordingly, has increased amazingly in the territories inhabited by the Masai, and the lions, nature's check on the increase of game, have grown in number proportionately.

Sometimes these wild beasts become an absolute pest to the Masai themselves. Then they go out, thirty or forty warriors equipped only with spear, sword, and shield. One morning they surround the place where the lion has torn an ox to pieces, and in a regular warriors' ecstasy they pursue, wear out, surround, and kill the maddened beast. A Masai in this almost hysterical state is braver, more reckless, and at the moment more dangerous than the lion he is attacking. He works himself up into a real fanatical ecstasy, foams at the mouth, brandishes his sword, and casts his spear, and one can easily imagine the terror which these fearless warriors evoked when, in past times, they attacked and always conquered their neighbors.

A Masai lion-hunt of this kind was intended to be the chief attraction of the Prince's three weeks' program.

His Royal Highness had many guests in his camp: there were the Governor and his wife, Sir Edward and Lady Grigg, Lord and Lady Delamere, my wife, Captain Ritchie, and others. The Prince wanted them all to see this hunt.

It was reported in the morning that four male lions were on the rhinoceros which had been shot the evening before when it attacked the Prince. The lions were watched; it was said that they had gone and lain down in the brushwood not far from the shot rhinoceros. This patch of brushwood was in the middle of open country, and four hundred yards away was a river-bed with trees, bushes, and undergrowth. A quarter of a mile farther on was a hillock which to some degree dominated the surrounding landscape.

So we all went out, and the specialists — Finch-Hatton, Ritchie, Lord Delamere, the Masai chief, and I — considered what the lions would do in their first panic, when they suddenly discovered the danger that threatened them. At the same time it had to be remembered that what mattered was not so much to kill the lions as to give the distinguished company the best possible idea of what a Masai lion-hunt with spears was really like.

We all put forward our proposals, and when the final decision was left to me, I agreed with the

"ONE OF THE TOUGHEST SPORTSMEN"

Masai chief. After all, it was his men who might possibly lose their lives, and it was his skill we were to see.

He divided his force into three groups. One was to prevent the lions from running down to the bed of the river, where the concealing bushes would make it impossible to see what was going on; another group was drawn up before the spectators on the hillock — this party, of course, was intended to dispatch the lions to the happy hunting-grounds — and the third group was to attack. This party, when the others had reached the posts allotted to them, was to approach the now sleeping lions and drive them out.

This was a skillful plan in theory; in practice it was completely ruined by the sporting enthusiasm and passion for the fray of the third group. The bonds of discipline did not hold. The men had promised their chief to obey his orders in every detail, but they forgot their promise in the excitement of battle. The old warriors' blood welled up — to attack and kill was their sole thought. Those ten men were delirious; nothing on earth could check them. When in their right mind, they had listened with approval to the exposition of the plan, but as soon as they caught sight of their mortal enemy, the slayer of cattle, this was all forgotten.

Before the two first groups had been able to take their places — indeed, long before the spectators had reached the hillock allotted to them — they had rushed headlong into the brushwood to get at the lions, brandishing their spears and yelling with excitement.

This ill-considered attack ended as badly as it deserved to; the four lions woke up and had time to place themselves in safety down in the donga, with its screening trees, dense undergrowth, and long grass. The chances of the party being able to watch the fight in detail were in the circumstances small — nothing could be seen from the hillock anyhow — so I collected all the cars as quickly as I could and had them driven down to the dried-up river-bed. The cars were parked, and then I placed the spectators on a sandy bank just in front of a small copse. I thought that one or more of the lions, pursued by the Masai, might perhaps try to find their way out here, and that the final battle would take place on this spot.

All the warriors were now among the bushes and undergrowth. Howls and yells mingled with the roaring of the lions. The brushwood swayed this way and that as though pulled about by a violent storm; now and then a spear-point gleamed in the sun, or a glimpse was caught of a yellowish, swiftly gliding body. More yells, more roars! We could hear and imagine the ferocious struggle, but we could see nothing — it was like sitting in a theater while a play is going on with the curtain lowered.

But the situation was not to the liking of the Prince of Wales. He had arranged for the play to be acted with the curtain up, and reckoned with the possibility of obtaining several yards of unique film, and before anyone could say a word he had suddenly plunged in among the bushes without any other weapon than his camera; Finch-Hatton and I had the greatest difficulty in following him.

A lion was speared not four yards away from him, but there was no possibility of making a film in such conditions.

The Masai, now absolutely raving, flung themselves on this lion. They waved their swords, danced with their spears, and within a quarter of an hour two male lions had been killed. A native had been bitten in the back, but the doctor we had brought with us attended him immediately. The injured man was taken to the hospital in an ambulance the same evening, and he was back with his tribe in a few days.

Tender towards wild creatures as he always is, the Prince did not wish us to hunt the remaining animals. The two speared lions, on the other hand, were borne in triumph to the camp, and there was a prolonged war-dance that evening round their dead bodies.

Before I leave this lion-hunt, I must relate a rather amusing incident which happened while we were in the bushes after the lions. I mentioned that I had left the spectators on a sandbank close to the donga, but that the Prince refused quietly to await the course of events, and that Finch-Hatton and I, who had rifles with us, had to follow him in among the warriors. Meanwhile one of the remaining lions came out of the brushwood and tried to jump up from the river-bed on to the bank, missed, fell down on its back, retreated a few steps, took another leap, and came up only a few yards from the spectators.

The latter, being unarmed, looked at the excited lion with some alarm and wondered what they should do. I was not there myself, but I heard from my wife that the situation might well have compared with the famous scene in which the lions are let loose upon the Christians in the Colosseum, and a tall, dignified fellow awaits his fate in the middle of the arena. Sir Edward Grigg was the brave man in this case, and I can well imagine the others grouped round him.

When we returned to the camp after the per-

"ONE OF THE TOUGHEST SPORTSMEN"

formance, a telegram awaited me. It was from Voi and told me that the elephant we had hunted during those hard and strenuous five days had now turned up again in the same region. It was decided at once that we should strike camp and go to Simba station, where the Prince's train was waiting.

But I had to be carried to the cars. I had had the bad luck to be suddenly attacked by acute malaria and could not stand on my legs. The Prince showed himself as helpful and thoughtful as usual and had me put into the compartment next his own. When the train reached Voi at six next morning and the Prince came to take my temperature, I made the disturbing discovery that malaria was announcing its presence in his own feverishly shining eyes.

"Your Royal Highness would do best to take your own temperature," I said. "My attack is nearly over."

I am sure the Prince was more surprised than I when he examined the thermometer and found that he had a temperature of 102 degrees. The engine-driver was immediately ordered to work up the highest possible steam pressure, and within a quarter of an hour we were on our way to the doctors and hospitals of Nairobi.

As a curiosity — and a compliment to the telegraph authorities — I may mention that the Prince sent a telegram from the train to his father in London, and an answer to that telegram arrived before the train, which was going pretty fast, had covered another sixty miles.

XV. *The Masai*

THE MASAI have been mentioned in this book in various connections. I should like to dwell on them for a few moments.

There is something in the chiseled features of their dark faces which tells us that these sinewy, stark-naked men, and their women overloaded with heavy ornaments, are not real Negroes.

No one knows exactly where they came from; from the north, the professors say, and it seems probable, for the Masai have not much in common with the Bantu peoples. Some say that, before our era opened, they pastured their flocks in northwestern Asia along with God's own people; and I recollect that among others the Swede Cardale

Luck, who has a farm up near Lumbwa, has published a book in which he thinks he can prove that they belong to one of the lost tribes of Israel.

Now they are thinly spread over a large area in Kenya and Tanganyika, from Mount Elgon in the north to about the center of what was German East Africa in the south. The boundaries to east and west mainly follow the Rift valley, though with a pretty wide margin.

There are a number of lakes within the region inhabited by the Masai — Lakes Nakuru, Naivasha, and Natron, for example — but the people of the steppes gaze at their blue surface, where the flamingoes swim in such masses that they look like lovely floating islands, without a gleam of interest. They have never been in a boat, have never tried their luck as fishermen; and the hippopotami's masses of meat and lard, which to other tribes are a heavenly blessing, leave them unmoved.

The Masai accompany their herds from one pasture-ground to another. There are, indeed, Masai who always live in the same place, but they are not many and are mainly concentrated in a few areas in Tanganyika — round Lake Natron and south of Mount Meru.

The other natives despise them, and fierce battles have been fought out between this agricultural tribe and the freebooters from the plains to the northward, who long knew no laws but their own. Now they are pacified, to use the current term. The *pax Britannica*, supported by the heavy tread of well-trained troops, has damped the warriors' zeal.

The young Masai have no longer any chance of frightening neighboring tribes out of their wits, stealing cattle, and striking ruthlessly at the enemy's wavering ranks. But the curious law still exists which bids the young men of the tribe live in a separate kraal from the age of fifteen to twenty-one, like a separate warrior caste, and the proverb survives from the golden age of unhindered forays: " If, when the sun sets, the sky is the color of blood, some warriors have made a successful raid."

Now the pugnacious warriors have to content themselves with talk of deeds long past or deeds intended, though the latter are mainly limited to spearing lions in the bush. But as lately as 1850 the Masai were considered a power to be reckoned with within the regions they called their own, and even the slave-dealers' well-equipped convoys drew aside respectfully before the pastoral tribe's advance.

Nowadays one often seen the young warriors — *Il muran* — talking outside the kraal, leaning on their spears, and standing on one leg with the other foot against the knee — a habit which they share with others among the diverse races of Africa.

But they have other habits which are unique.

No man or woman who wishes to be considered a true Masai will touch the flesh of game. The speared lion's mane is used as a head ornament, as it is by the Abyssinians farther north, and when the hunter has killed a gnu he takes only the tail with which to brush away the flies or keep intrusive fleas on the move. Beef and milk are their favorite food and drink, the latter sometimes mixed with blood; I have seen warriors open their oxen's veins and drink the warm foaming blood. It can fairly be said that their diet seems well suited to their occupation.

These young warriors, *Il muran*, have one great privilege. The young unmarried girls may go to their kraal; so that a low but perhaps agreeable standard of morality prevails. The consequence, too, is that the women's fidelity after marriage is often extremely doubtful.

This rather curious custom should perhaps be seen against the background of a legend, which I quote from a book:[1]

[1] A. C. Hollis: *The Masai, Their Language and Folklore*. Quoted by courtesy of the Oxford University Press.

THE MASAI

"There once lived an old man who had two daughters and a son. In course of time the children grew up and the boy became a warrior.

"War then broke out between the old man's people and a neighbouring tribe, with the result that the former feared to take their cattle to the salt-lick, as they were accustomed to do once or twice a month. The cattle suffered in consequence and gave no milk.

"When the old man's son saw that his cattle were falling ill he made up his mind to take them to the salt-lick, and to die with them if necessary. His elder sister accompanied him, and as he was leaving the paternal roof, he told his younger sister that if she saw smoke issuing from the watering-place, she might know that he was safe.

"On his arrival at the salt-lick he erected his kraal and encircled it with a hedge of thorns. The next morning he took his cattle out to graze, leaving his sister to look after the kraal. For some days the enemy did not come near them, but one morning they suddenly appeared. The girl was alone at the time, and they made love to her, after which they departed.

"On the warrior's return in the evening he noticed the footmarks, but said nothing to his sister. The next morning he drove his cattle out to graze as usual, and when he had taken them to a safe distance, he returned and hid himself near the kraal. The enemy came again and made love to the girl.

When they were about to leave, the warrior heard his sister say to them: 'If you come this evening I will sing when my brother milks the big cow. You can then take me away and the cattle too.'

"The warrior went back to his cattle, and in the evening when he had returned to the kraal, he placed his weapons in readiness, and pretended to milk the big cow. His sister at once commenced to sing, so he left the cow, and seized his weapons. Almost at the same time one of the enemy jumped over the thorn hedge, only to be killed by the warrior. Five others met with the same fate, and the remainder fled. The warrior then sallied forth, and collected a lot of firewood, with which he lit a fire and burnt the bodies.

"It had been raining, and the women of the old man's kraal were repairing the damage done to their huts by plastering them with a mixture of cow-dung and clay. The warrior's younger sister was on the roof of the hut, and when she saw the smoke issuing from the salt-lick, she cried out: 'My brother is safe.' She was asked how she knew, and she told everybody what her brother had said to her when he left them.

"The next morning all the people of the old man's kraal moved to the salt-lick, and their cattle speedily recovered. The warrior related what his sister had done, and her father sought out a man to marry her.

"Before this event it was not customary for the

THE MASAI

young girls to go to the warriors' kraals, and they remained at home till they were married; but when the story of the girl's treachery was known, it was considered safer to let them go, and sing and dance and live with the warriors. And this custom has been observed ever since."

That his woman shall bear him a number of children seems to the Masai as natural a thing as the milking of the cows at evening, and her barrenness, and that alone, will give rise to profound speculations concerning the evil spirits that play their pranks in the dusk. All are agreed that witchery and devilment must be the causes, and the only question is whether the powers of evil can be propitiated or exorcized.

Not even death is the subject of many gloomy meditations; the Masai do not fear the man with the sharp scythe. Men die, are annihilated — what more? The hyenas have only to do their duty. Only when one of the chiefs of the tribe dies, or its medicine-man (a very powerful person who should in no circumstances be confused with the ordinary quacks), is a certain scanty ritual to be noted at the burial — for these are the only people who are buried in the ground. It is believed that after death their souls go into some snake, and the women may sometimes be seen offering milk even to the dreaded black mamba outside the fence of the kraal.

The boys are circumcised at about fifteen, and it is considered particularly unbecoming for them to show the slightest sign of fear or suffering during the painful operation. If they do, the whole family is disgraced. It often happens that the parents, full of uneasy apprehension, disappear in good time in order not to be exposed to the scoffs of their friends if their son's courage should fail him.

A similar operation is performed on the girls before they marry, and they immediately show the change which has taken place in their lives by adorning their ears and neck with heavy iron rings.

Marriage is preceded by long and elaborate ceremonies, of which the slaughtering of one or several oxen is an important part. The man buys his wife, paying for her in cattle, and polygamy is the rule, as among most of the African tribes.

In the history of the Masai as known to them — that is, since about a hundred years ago, for oral tradition goes no farther back — two events of the greatest importance to the race have occurred.

The first was the struggle between the resident

and the nomad tribes; the second the arrival of Europeans in their country. This white invasion in particular was fatal to the Masai, especially as, on the principle that misfortunes never come singly, it was accompanied by a devastating cattle plague and a severe epidemic of smallpox. The surrounding blacks, who for decades had suffered severely from the Masai raids, were not slow to take advantage of their neighbors' enfeebled state and fall upon and slaughter the now more or less defenseless people and their cattle. The numbers of the Masai were severely reduced; the tribe never regained its former power, and now probably numbers little more than fifty thousand.

Much of their old land has been divided among European farmers, who are not particularly pleased to have the Masai herds grazing in the neighborhood, for rinderpest often comes with them. Several attempts have been made to induce the blacks to comply with the regulations of the medical authorities at Nairobi, especially as regards the introduction of disinfecting baths for beasts — " cattle dips " — but without any notable result. The Masai are of opinion that what they do not know about cattle-breeding is not worth knowing.

I remember an occasion when the Masai from

near and far assembled at Narok at the summons of Sir Edward Northey, then Governor of Kenya. They came in multitudes, led by their chiefs, and at the head of them all was the old medicine-man Sendeyo.

The Governor made a long and excellent speech. He pointed out, among other things, the desirability of the Masai making roads, sending their sons to school in order that they might learn to read and write, constructing regulation cattle dips, and otherwise complying with the ordinances of the medical authorities.

Not a muscle of the warriors' hard faces was seen to move during the long speech. When it was over Sendeyo stepped forward.

He replied that since the Government wished it they would build roads, though no one could understand what was the use of it, seeing that they had got on without such things from time immemorial. The trodden paths, mountains, hills, and rivers were road enough and guide enough for the man who knew his country. They would also send their sons to school to learn the art of reading and writing, but only because the white man wished it, and although such learning was certainly heavier to bear than bow and spear and shield. The latter, moreover, had been proved to be good, practical things; the former was of no use. But the Masai would never construct any cattle dips, for he, Sendeyo, knew more about cattle diseases than fifty white men.

Then Sir Edward Northey spoke of Lord Delamere, whom they all knew and whose herds were greater than the Masai's own, although the beasts were stronger and better and sired by European bulls. He always " dipped " his cows, and the cattle were healthy and continually increasing.

Sendeyo replied, with dignity and without hesitation:

" When we could graze our herds on Lord Delamere's land, in old days, we never lost a cow from plague either."

It is not worth while to argue with such people.

No, the white men's laws do not suit pastoral people from the north. Look at their huts, their naked young men, and their women overloaded with heavy ornaments. No one knows how long they will follow their herds along the Rift valley and over the endless plateaus which their wild, bloodthirsty forefathers once called theirs. If they will not take the road which leads from the thorn bushes of the desert to the tended garden of culture, their days are numbered; but one of their proverbs will always hold good: " Bravery is not everything, and however brave a man may be, two brave men are better."

No one has cast doubt upon the Masai's courage, but the forces against them are overwhelming.

XVI. *Crocodiles and Hippopotami*

A FEW years ago I had pitched my temporary camp by Lakes Baringo and Hannigan in Kenya. I was assisting a moving-picture expedition which had made it its task to film the amazingly rich bird life which flourishes there among the hippopotami and crocodiles.

I had the opportunity of making many interesting observations; but I remember particularly one morning when I had gone out at dawn to conceal myself in the reeds opposite a sandbank and watch animal life at the moment when the crocodiles crawl up on the sand to rest in the morning sunshine after their night's fishing.

First they come floating like tree-trunks on the

surface of the water; they lie still for some time till they have made sure that no danger is at hand. Then a big crocodile, a twelve-foot giant, crawls out. He walks slowly and stumblingly on his weak legs, lies on his stomach, and opens his jaws, which get fixed, so that they remain open even when he is asleep. The gray-speckled crocodile birds come hopping up; they flutter round, approach carefully, and, with a dentist's skill, pick out of the sleeping monster's jaws all the fragments of food which have become lodged during the night's meal.

Suddenly a hippopotamus poked his bright brown head up out of the water, winked once or twice with his little eyes, pushed his head farther out, looked hard at the crocodile on the sandbank, climbed up slowly, and quietly emerged on the sand. He stood looking about him in the warm sun and then slowly approached the crocodile, which closed his jaws suddenly, although the birds had not completed his morning tooth-brushing. The hippopotamus went right up to the crocodile and gave him one blow across the tail with his great head. The crocodile turned round and hissed at the insolent disturber of the peace; but the hippopotamus quietly took another step forward and, with a swiftness of which one would not have thought the clumsy beast capable, gave the giant crocodile a fresh blow with his head amidships, which flung the monster, certainly four hundred pounds in weight, out into the lake like a pebble.

I never saw anything like it before or since, and to this day I cannot understand what sudden impulse seized the hippopotamus. It is not easy to imagine any cause of enmity between hippopotamus and crocodile; they have no common interests, either in the water or on land, which would seem likely to collide and create discord between them. On the whole it seems probable that the hippopotamus's behavior was inspired simply by bad temper, or a desire to demonstrate his strength and his contempt.

I saw another curious sight that same day. Two hippopotami climbed up on the sandbank, which was fairly high, and began to play. They pushed each other, snapped at each other like horses at play, and rose on their hind legs like rearing stallions; but the effort was too great — they both fell sideways down the steep slope into the lake, so that a huge splash of water rose skywards and the water was disturbed for several hundred yards around.

The blacks show extreme caution when they go in their ramshackle craft on waters where hippopotami exist. The following little episode may serve to show how great the danger really is. Once, when hunting for a few days on the Nile, I had been delayed, and in order to catch the boat which was to meet me at Rhino Camp I had to try to persuade the chief Mutir to give me his best canoe and his best rowers to paddle me there by night. The man refused. It had taken him months to get the fine boat, and he thought there was small likelihood of our escaping the hippopotami by night. But after long persuasion — and high payment — I succeeded at last in persuading him to give me a smaller boat with six paddlers, and off we went on an eight hours' trip, full of excitement and danger, for the hippopotami were neighing and snorting all night both in the water and on the banks. That nothing happened was entirely due to the rowers' awe of the colossal beasts and their consequent ability to paddle along by night absolutely noiselessly. Luckily the night was so clear that the men could distinguish the shapes of the hippopotami's heads sticking up out of the water like little bright-shining islets. We all knew what would happen if we made an error in navigation and ran upon one of them.

Apropos of being late, one of the most glorious trips I have ever made on the Nile was when I and two friends missed the boat at Butiaba. We had

CROCODILES AND HIPPOPOTAMI

to borrow the Governor's gig, a light craft with ten oars, and row the ninety miles' distance from Butiaba across Lake Albert and so down the Nile. The ten boys sang in time to their even strokes. We followed the course of the river, cooked our meals when we were hungry, and slept when we felt inclined. There were crocodiles in masses on the sandbanks. We shot as many as we could of those obnoxious poachers of fish and beasts alike. Many historical memories cling to those reaches of the river, and when one has read the books of the earlier explorers and adventurers who pushed their way into these wilds with countless difficulties, fighting against fever, hostile natives, slave-dealers, and wild beasts, one's imagination easily gets to work.

In waters like these, swarming with fierce crocodiles, bathing is of course out of the question. Even the black man approaches the river-bank with the greatest caution when he has to fetch water or drink. The crocodile attacks like a shot — the quickness of the apparently awkward creature is incredible; he shoots forward as swiftly as a torpedo. He rushes up the bank where the black man is sitting and with one blow of his tail sweeps the victim out into the water, where he is immediately bitten to death or first drowned. If one slits up the belly of an old crocodile, one often finds some memento of past tragedies in the form of necklaces or bracelets.

I was once with George Vanderbilt in the neighborhood of Entebbe, on Lake Victoria. We were fishing there for the Philadelphia Museum and had hundreds of yards of nets of different sizes laid out for this purpose. We had with us, too, several collapsible boats, and a rubber boat which could be blown up. One evening, when we were taking up our nets, Vanderbilt in the rubber boat was the last man out on the lake. I was already having my evening bathe when he came in. A few minutes later a boy came running and shouted out that there was a big crocodile splashing most horribly down by the landing-stage. I declared in a few well-chosen words that I did not care in the least. But when I went down to the landing-stage next morning to row out to the nets, the rubber boat had disappeared — only a few scanty strips of rubber lay at the bottom of the lake close to the stage. The splashing crocodile had carried off the rest. The crocodile had no doubt been on the watch and followed Vanderbilt and had hoped that he was still in the boat when it attacked.

In the same regions lives an old and large crocodile named Lutembe. The natives regard it as sacred for some reason or other, and it has grown so tame that when they call: " Lutembe! Lutembe! " it comes up and waits quietly for its customary meal of fish.

We spent hour after hour and day after day at the place I have mentioned, filming a herd of elephants which lived there. We gradually got to know almost every elephant. The largest of all was an elephant with only one tusk. We naturally christened him " One Tusk." Then we had George and Charlie, smaller bulls, both obstinate rivals for the favors of One Tusk's large herd of cows and young heifers.

One day One Tusk lost his patience with young Master George, who had been more than usually daring in his approach to one of One Tusk's ladies. George was chased out of the herd with furious trumpetings, nor was One Tusk satisfied till he had seen his rival to a safe distance. Then he went back to his companions and stood quietly twitching his ears until George again dared to approach. George now played the penitent; he walked slowly, nosed about, and here and there plucked a bit of greenery from some bush as if nothing had happened. But One Tusk did not seem to be at all too sure of young George's repentant mood; he approached him with ears extended. But George defied the danger; he boldly went up to his senior and laid his trunk on the side of One Tusk's head, as much as to say: " Forgive me; I'll be good now." One Tusk replied by laying his trunk on the other's head — pardon was granted. Then they returned to the herd side by side.

But let me return to the crocodiles and hippopotami. The reader can hardly imagine the masses of these creatures that one sees in the Victoria Nile just below the Murchison Falls. Of all the rivers in the world the Nile contains most fish per cubic yard of water. The Nile fish, like all others, work up against the stream. The Murchison Falls, with their colossal mass of water rushing down a steep slope seventy-five feet high, are too severe an obstacle; the fish get no farther than the pool below the falls, and there they remain in a black mass, fin to fin. This pool is the crocodiles' paradise. They lie there in the blazing sun in thousands; it is an absolute nightmare to see them rolling from the bank into the river below.

The place is creepy-crawly with tens of thousands of the ugly reptiles. They lie in the water as close-packed as sardines in a box; if they grow hungry they have only to open their mouths.

Masses of hippopotami, too, are to be seen in this welter of crocodiles and fish. Head after head pops

CROCODILES AND HIPPOPOTAMI

up out of the water; they wink their little eyes, open their jaws in a gigantic yawn, and neigh in untroubled peace.

This place is undoubtedly one of the things most worth seeing in Africa, protected as it is by effective legislation. No gunshot may disturb its peace. Great herds of elephants wander about; buffaloes are seen everywhere; pretty waterbuck and graceful cob antelopes graze on the river-banks. It is an animal park unequaled in any other part of the globe, and the public can get there twice a month by the comfortable steamers of the Uganda Railway, which start from Butiaba, on the eastern shore of Lake Albert.

XVII. *Fishing*

BEFORE I begin my chapter on fishing, I ought to say that my knowledge of the subject is nothing to boast of. As a fisherman I am an amateur — certainly a much interested amateur, but an amateur all the same. But if I can have my will, I mean to get a boat and try to discover the secrets of the till now unexplored deep-sea fishing off the coast washed by the Indian Ocean, and perhaps I should have been wiser to put off writing about fishing till I had that experience behind me. But, on the other hand, I think this book would be in a way incomplete if I did not — if only very briefly — say something about my adventures in boats with men like Hemingway and Sir Charles Markham.

FISHING

If a fisherman in the Stockholm skerries hauls up a perch weighing two pounds he cannot sleep all night for pride, and I personally would rather avoid all intercourse with him for some little time after his " exploit." If I were obliged to talk to him, I should advise him to travel to Africa and fish for Nile perch. They weigh a bit more! A Nile perch weighing two hundred pounds is no rarity, and do not think that its size makes it poor eating! On the contrary. The Nile perch — or *buta*, as it is called in Lake Albert, and *capitaine* in Belgian and French waters — is considered an extreme delicacy, and I can guarantee that it is.

Both the Nile perch and the tiger fish — another fish which the cook is glad to see in the pot — are plentiful in the lake I have just mentioned, but the Nile perch does not occur in Lake Victoria. To make up for this, there is an abundance of other edible fish, and there is no question that the development of the fishing industry in recent years has in many places revolutionized the domestic economy of the natives. The trains are now made up with strings of refrigerator cars for the fish, and quantities have been smoked since it has been found that the natives like the taste of smoked fish.

In the mountain streams, where the temperature of the water is low enough to allow the spawn to hatch, trout have been introduced by the Government and have settled down astonishingly well. There is hardly a river now in the Aberdare mountains or the Kenya highlands which does not afford excellent opportunities for the sport-loving fisherman with rod and fly. Fishing for sport in these regions requires a stronger emphasis on the word " sport " than anywhere else in the world — owing to the danger to which the fisherman is always exposed from aggressive rhinoceroses and buffaloes. I have a vague recollection of having seen this headline over a news paragraph in a paper: " Killed by rhinoceros while trout-fishing," and it does not sound so bad.

The deep-sea fishing on the coast is — as I mentioned just now — practically unexplored. The facilities required for deep-water fishing for sport in the high seas which often prevail in the Indian Ocean do not at present exist. The author Ernest Hemingway, perhaps one of the best-known fishermen in America, tried a week's fishing here two years ago with Alfred Vanderbilt and Philip Percival and was able to form a particularly good idea of the possibilities of the coast. In that week he caught a sail-fish weighing nearly a hundred pounds, and thought he had proof of the presence of tunny, swordfish, and marlin.

FISHING

In the summer of 1935 I had a month's fishing as Hemingway's guest at Bimini in the Bahamas and got the fascination of the sport into my blood. To hold on to and tire out a gigantic fish, weighing as much as a ton, with a rod and a comparatively slender line, is a test of both strength and endurance. To every movement of the fish the fisherman must react with a skill which requires many years of training and experience. The unforgettable month during which my wife and I basked in the sun on these daily fishing expeditions did not, of course, make me a trained fisherman, but it gave me an idea of the extraordinary interest of deep-sea fishing as a sport, and to what a test one's qualities as a seaman, physical strength, and special knowledge are put. For it the very best apparatus and a boat with an absolutely reliable engine are required. As the Congo forests conceal what are perhaps the largest elephants in the world, though they are hard to find, the depths of ocean swarm with fish of enormous dimensions. They exist everywhere, but only the expert knows at what depth and how far from land they are to be found and what currents are the most favorable.

To give the reader some idea of what a struggle with a fish of this kind means, I should like to describe our last lay at Bimini. "Up with the sun" is a rule for fishermen all the world over, and the sun had not long been above the horizon when we found what we wanted — a few smallish tunnies of about six pounds each to use as bait. Then we went up and down the outer deep-water line in the boat — a big sea-going ten-ton motor-boat.

In a little while we got a very strong bite. The fish went right down to the bottom, and the reel whizzed round at a fearful speed. Yard after yard of line ran out, but finally Hemingway put on the brake, though he gave way a little now and then. At last the fish stopped rushing and the fight began.

Hemingway is a gigantic fellow weighing, I am sure, over a hundred and ninety pounds, with shoulders like a wrestler and a chest like Hercules. With the big, strong Hardy rod quivering under the colossal forces at work on both sides, he slowly began to haul in. But the fish did not give way. It was as though the hook had become fastened to the sea-bottom.

And now the foam began to hiss about the heavy boat's stem; we were being towed out to sea at a good pace. Hemingway toiled at reel and line like a galley-slave at his oar. The sweat stood in drops on his bare back as he strained every muscle to hold

NATIVE FISHERMEN ON AN AFRICAN LAKE

AN ALARMING CHARGE

and tire out his quarry. What could it be? A tunny, a swordfish, or perhaps a giant marlin? We had to pour water over his back from time to time to freshen him up a bit.

After an hour and three quarters the fish slowly gave way, the reel began to move again, the line was hauled in yard by yard, and soon we saw, deep down in the crystal-clear water, a silvery-gleaming, hovering fish. It was still too far down for us to be able to distinguish what it was, but now at last it was coming up!

A shark! A disgusting giant shark, of the hammer-headed species — I am sorry, but I have no idea what its Latin name is. There was great disappointment and annoyance on board; when one goes out lion-hunting one is not pleased to get a hyena, and the shark is the hyena of the seas, but a much greater annoyance to the fishermen than the four-legged hyena to the hunters. It frequently happens that the shark snatches its prey from the hook on the way up to the surface, and if it does not get the whole it always takes a bit.

The shark over which Hemingway had almost worked himself to death had not swallowed the bait, but by chance had got the hook caught in one of its front fins. It had fought for its life so strenuously, however — that it had died of heart failure. Even our friend Hemingway was, as I have already indicated, half dead; but we doused him generously with cold water and poured a strong brandy down his throat, and he was soon all right again.

XVIII. *The River Congo and Lake Chad*

SOME time in the early spring of 1927, I think it was, Sir Charles Markham asked me if I felt inclined to take a motor-boat trip up the Congo and then up the Ubangi to the town of Bangi. Thence we were to travel overland with the boat to the river Shari, which we would follow till it ran out into Lake Chad. The program was attractive; I accepted, and so we began a journey which was not quite free from hazardous adventures.

From the Congo to Bangi the journey was pleasant enough, apart from its monotony. We went slowly up against the stream, and the forest-clothed banks offered little variety during the three weeks it took us to reach Bangi. Our boat was heavily loaded and had two smaller boats in tow, so we could not go at racing speed.

At Bangi the difficulties began. We had to get the boat across from the river Ubangi to the river Shari, a distance of about 250 miles, but on closer investigation it was found that there was no wheeled vehicle large and strong enough to carry our five-ton steel boat over. After many troubles we succeeded in making an arrangement which enabled us to drop the boat into the river Shari, but the sigh of relief we drew was certainly a little premature. The motor had not been working an hour before disaster was upon us in the shape of a stout, low, overhanging branch which caught fast in the cover of the boat. No more was needed. The boat heeled over, the cargo shifted further, the water streamed in, and a few moments later the whole concern was at the bottom of the river. Only a faint ripple on the surface showed where our craft had sunk.

It had gone to the bottom with all we had. Photographic apparatus, twelve thousand feet of film, rifles, provisions — in short, everything that an expedition of the kind must have for a four months' trip remote from all civilization had been lost. We certainly succeeded in raising the boat after ten days' hard work, but the greater part of our equipment was completely destroyed, and we had to telegraph to Europe for new gear.

Then we began the journey downstream again, poling our way along, as our Ford motor, which was driven by dry batteries, of course refused to function. It was a whole month before we again heard the welcome sound of the motor. Luckily we had been able to kill the time by shooting. There are masses of waterfowl on the river, geese and duck and waders of all kinds. On the banks are to be seen cob antelopes and waterbuck, and farther inland are excellent hunting-grounds, where we killed Derby elands, roan antelopes, buffaloes, a few elephants, a couple of rhinoceroses, and two lions — all for the Natural History Museum in Kensington. The museum had further commissioned us to investigate the local fish and take home representatives of the various species that occur. We had, I may say parenthetically, the pleasure of contributing to the discovery of no less than four new kinds.

We used to tie up at night alongside some inviting sandbank and lived on the whole an ideally leisurely and interesting life. I could fill pages with experiences and observations made on the journey down towards the estuary, but the above jottings will have to suffice for the present. Lake Chad gave us a friendly welcome; we crossed successfully to the smiling archipelago in the northern part of the lake — thousands of islands which offer good pasturage to the natives' great herds of cattle.

Curiously enough, the grazing is managed in much the same way as on the islands in the northern Stockholm skerries. When the grass on one island is all eaten up for the time being, the cattle are transferred to the next, but instead of the cattle ferries at home, the natives have cork pegs. They are used as a kind of float, and with their help the natives get over from island to island, the cattle swimming behind. Both people and cattle in these parts move in the water as if they were web-footed; one can see long lines of women swimming across to the next island with the children firmly fastened to their heads, despite the fact that the lake is full of crocodiles. There seems to be a tacit agreement between the two parties to leave one another in peace.

The cattle on these islands are much bigger than those one meets in Kenya. They have colossal horns as much as ten inches in diameter, and when they swim from island to island with heads thrown back, it is said that these horns help to keep their muzzles above the water.

The secret of the primitiveness of transport conditions is the lack of timber. We are here on the edge of the Sahara. The vegetation is very scanty — there are no trees to be hollowed out for canoes. For journeys of any length Viking-like rafts of hard bundles of papyrus, bound together, are constructed; and in these vessels even voyages across the great lake are undertaken. Obviously these must soon fall to pieces — but a lot *that* matters! The natives simply put together a new papyrus boat.

We fished and hunted in these parts for a month and then returned across the lake to Fort Lamy, where we sold the boat and bought a three-quarter-ton International motor-truck, with which we entered on a hazardous voyage over the then little-known sand deserts of the Sahara.

"Misfortunes seldom come singly," said Sir Charles when the boat had spun round in the river Shari. He referred to Bobo, who had been pleased to join us when we were busy fishing up the sunk vessel. But he did not mean it unkindly; I am sure he was very fond of Bobo, and so was I, and so were all the others. And Bobo was one of those who improve on closer acquaintance — he was pleasant and sociable and had many amusing and original tricks.

Bobo was a half-grown chimpanzee, who cherished a burning passion for travel by boat. On the journey down the river he used to spend the days in the smaller of the boats we towed, where he sat proudly on the after thwart, closely watching all that took place on the banks. He kept an especially sharp look-out for the baboons and small monkeys in the trees — it was, among other reasons, on account of the baboons that we had to keep him fastened on a long chain, for if he had got loose among them they would undoubtedly have bitten him to death.

I shall never forget his expression once when he forgot his chain and tried to jump up on a branch which was passing over the boat. He wanted to show off and demonstrate that he could look after himself in a matter of that kind. But in the very moment of triumph he felt the chain tighten; an expression of terror came into his eyes that I shall never forget — and he did not repeat the attempt.

Bobo's love of boats was equaled by his detestation of motor-cars. When we began to test the motor-truck at Fort Lamy he ran away and hid, showing the strongest signs of fear, and when we were really going to drive off he grew so terrified that he was trembling all over when we lifted him up to the top.

But once there, he seemed to settle down pretty well.

While we were at Fort Lamy he lived in the back yard, chained to a shady tree. Hundreds of curious Arabs and Tuaregs came to look at him every day, but we did not let them inside the walls, afraid that Bobo would become frightened and unruly. They invented a good game, however. The Arabs threw stones at Bobo, which he returned with an astonishing accuracy of aim, so that they had to bob down hurriedly behind the wall. He gave a proof of the chimpanzee's reasoning power and cunning when he jumped up, took careful aim at an Arab who was looking at him from one end of the wall, and then, quick as lightning, flung the stone at a man who was standing at the opposite corner, and who, to Bobo's immeasurable delight, was hit plumb on the head.

One day Bobo managed to get loose — the fact was that, possibly with the help of some Arab boy, he wriggled out of his collar and went out for a walk in the town. With unfailing intuition, he went into the main street and began to chase the terrified natives for fun. All attempts to capture him proved fruitless, and things reached a point at which it was a question whether we should not be obliged to shoot him. But late in the afternoon I succeeded in tempting him with a few splendid bananas, which are very rare in those parts. For all eventualities, I had my hippopotamus-hide whip hidden under my coat and the collar and chain in readiness in my pocket.

He succeeded in taking the first banana from me before I could catch him, but when he stretched out his paw for the next I caught hold of one of his arms, and a fearful struggle began. Bobo was large and powerful, nearly as strong as I was, and we rolled over and over in the street. The inhabitants shrieked and yelled. Bobo bit me through the left arm so that the blood squirted in all directions, but I had now got a grip of his throat and gave him a good thrashing with the hippopotamus-hide whip. I managed by degrees to get the collar and chain on him, but I did not leave him till he had calmed down, given me his paw, and begged my pardon.

I had the wounds bandaged at the hospital. It was found that a probe could be driven through the fleshy part of the forearm in two places. Bobo did not really mean any harm, but chimpanzees sometimes become completely hysterical and do not know what they are doing.

Poor Bobo died some time later — of the aftermath of an attack of inflammation of the lungs which he caught on the journey through the Congo forest home to my farm in Tanganyika.

Catherine was the name of a little miss chimpanzee, two years old, whom I once bought in the Congo. Catherine had been brought up with a little reddish-brown monkey with a white tip to its nose. She kept the monkey on a string and had done so for a whole year. At night they slept in each other's arms. Now and then the monkey succeeded in getting away from its patroness and running up the nearest tree, and it was most exciting to follow the furious chase which began when Catherine tried to recapture her lady companion — in which she always succeeded. When I got to Nairobi I presented Catherine and the monkey to Lady MacMillan, who built them a magnificent house, but unhappily Catherine soon sickened and died of scurvy, a very uncommon disease in an animal of the kind. After that the little monkey was allowed to live the rest of its life in freedom, but alone.

XIX. *Our Sahara Trip*

THE GOVERNOR of Fort Lamy, after a close inspection of the car which Markham had bought, took up a very skeptical attitude towards the Sahara trip which we had planned. He knew his desert and shook his head. The tires were too narrow. Where was the extra low gear which was indispensable if we were to force our way through miles of sand a foot deep? Did we realize that the month of April was the special time of strong winds and sandstorms, and that most of the water-holes were dried up then?

No, we knew nothing at all about it.

Well, at any rate, we might have heard of the Atlas mountains on the other side of the Sahara, where robber bands still operated audaciously on the borders of civilization? This alone ought to be enough to make us abstain from an attempt which, in his opinion, was doomed to failure.

We hesitated. But the unknown called to us powerfully from the desert, and adventure beckoned to us from behind the rolling dunes on the horizon. We had often followed where it led.

Our route ran due west along sandy tracks, through the outermost tip of what was the German Cameroons to Kano.

We rested there for three days and completed the car's outfit. The heavy International truck, three quarters of a ton in weight, which had been brought from Nairobi by the company's representative, Mr. King, had run irreproachably throughout the journey and was still in first-class condition. Only a few small changes had to be made.

The original tires, which strangely enough had never had a puncture since the journey began, were taken off to be used as spares, and the car had new thick rubber shoes put on all four feet. Proper water-, gasoline-, and oil-tanks were constructed and the motor thoroughly inspected. Our personal equipment was reduced to a minimum — two small suitcases holding thirty pounds each. We also took with us cameras, films, rifles, ammunition, and provisions and a black servant named Ali.

AFRICAN HUNTER

Kano is the biggest city in Africa, with not less than 500,000 inhabitants, but there has been no change to speak of in the architecture during the last few centuries. The houses of sun-dried brick mostly have flat roofs, and the streets are paved only here and there. The wanderer would think that he had been carried back to the Middle Ages but for the multitude of telephone wires and electric street lights which contrast sharply with the dreamy Eastern atmosphere that enwraps the town, for all its activity. The hot desert wind sweeps through the narrow alleys, and through the swarm of Arabian merchants and Negroes of every shade move, slowly and with dignity, mail-clad men of the Houssa tribe.

They have good, fast horses of the Arab type, and one day, when we had grown tired of watching the mechanics fiddling with the interior of the car, we went outside the town wall — an earth wall more than two miles long — to watch the races and other sports which were being held just at the time of our visit. Quite good fields turned out for the races, both for camels and horses, but the course was rather wider than what we are accustomed to at home — the desert is a spacious racetrack, if not an ideal one. For one race 450 horses started; the dust whirled up in huge clouds, blew into the spectators' faces, and filled noses, eyes, and ears. We could see nothing at all of the race — we heard only the clatter of hoofs; but a few hundred yards away a little gray horse emerged from the ruck, shot forward like an arrow, and won "hands down." On our way home we photographed the animal, an Arab stallion with good points, considerably smaller than most of the runners.

At one o'clock on the morning of March 27 everything was at last ready for our departure; the engine was started, and we rolled out of peaceful Kano. A train was standing in the station, and the locomotive blew out a large cloud of white smoke with a hissing noise. We took the road that led northward to Zinder.

The drive to Zinder passed off without a hitch, and we felt peculiarly cheerful. If it was no worse than this everything would go swimmingly — but the real desert had not begun yet. The commander of the troops quartered at Zinder was a pleasant fellow, who helped us with word and deed and marked out our route for the next few days on the map. He advised us first to drive westward to Niamey and then follow the course of the Niger to Gao, where the caravan route northward starts.

We reached the capital of the Niger colony on March 30 after a journey that involved little hardship. It had certainly been rather warm, about 112 degrees in the shade, and one could easily have boiled eggs in the water in the radiator, but there was no serious complaint to make against the roads. It was otherwise after we left Niamey. The sand lay a foot deep along our route, which was modestly marked out with little stone cairns.

To judge from the pretty red winding line marked on the map, the road between Kano and Gao should have been fairly uniform in character, but in reality, as I have said, it was otherwise. The desert winds met us, scorching hot, and swept the light sand together in deep drifts which at times completely buried the unimposing cairns that marked the route.

We wriggled along at a speed of ten miles an hour, and often had to stop to find the way.

We definitely lost it in the afternoon, and after a long and fruitless search decided to camp on the spot for the night. But we got no sleep to speak of, for some lions kept up a loud and cheerful conversation all night in the immediate neighborhood of the car. We trotted out into the sand in a sour morning humor, while Ali was cooking a Spartan breakfast, found the way almost at once, and arrived at Gao the same afternoon.

Photo, Viscountess Furness

MURCHERSON'S FALLS, VICTORIA NILE

A SAHARA FORTRESS

Gao was no metropolis. Apart from the necessary buildings — or barracks, if you like, for the troops are quartered there — the town consisted of three houses in all, plus a quantity of native huts. Since then Gao has become the terminus for the big buses of the Trans-Sahara Company and has grown enormously. When I visited the place again last year I found it quite unrecognizable, with its imposing streets, hotels, automobile workshops, and large aerodrome.

West of Gao lies Timbuktu, once the biggest market in Central Africa. Now, since the railway from Lagos to Kano has drawn to the last-named place the whole trade from the inner and northern Sahara, it is a dying town. The bazaars of Timbuktu are deserted, and scarcely any vehicles disturb the fowls which now regard the streets as their own. Certainly the French keep a fair-sized military detachment there, and a force of airplanes is in readiness to keep in check the robber bands which from time to time make their raids from the Gold Coast, to the great detriment of peaceful caravans and rather less pacific Tuaregs; but the garrison is not much in evidence, and in any case it cannot remove the impression of desolate emptiness which Timbuktu makes. People have gone, and thousands of storks have come in their place; men and officers are transferred; only Father Yakuba, the old white monk of Timbuktu, remains, for he loves his town, knows all there is to know about it, and in the course of time has become to tourists an attraction of the same international rank as the leaning tower of Pisa.

At Gao we got permission to replenish our stock of gasoline from the Government store, promising to repay later the amount of the precious liquid we had taken, and the commandant was also kind enough to secure us a guide who could accompany us half-way to our next destination, Tabankort. It was said that we should find a water-hole there and another ten miles farther north.

So off we started with the Governor of Dakar's pass in our pocket — " at your own risk and peril." The track at first wound among thorny bushes, and after we had parted from our guide, and later Tabankort had been sighted, the open desert lay around us on all sides, yellowish gray and silent.

How this now abandoned outpost on the borders of the Sahara could ever have been inhabited is a riddle to me. My friend Charles Markham, who stoically kept his diary through all the hardships of our journey and has allowed me to quote from it, wrote:

OUR SAHARA TRIP

"The heat defies all description and the water is almost as salt as sea-water. We decided not to fill our large water-tank, as according to information we had received at Gao we should pass another well ten miles farther north. But we filled our two smaller tins which were fastened to the running-board. We had to pour more water into the radiator every mile on account of the intense heat. We continued our journey; we found no friendly cairns, only old tracks of six-wheeled cars belonging to the Trans-Sahara Company, which run across the desert when passengers are willing to risk their lives. They carry a complete wireless equipment. . . .

"At a number of places the tracks could hardly be distinguished, and at midday we had still found no water-hole, but we went on, thinking that perhaps our informant had made a mistake about the distance. At 6.30 we came to the conclusion either that we had driven past the well or that the track did not lead to it. We had, therefore, to choose between two alternatives — either to return to Tabankort to get water, which actually meant driving back to Gao, since we had not petrol enough to start again from Tabankort, or to go on. We had only about three gallons of water left. Ali was by this time reduced to a mass of helpless flesh; he lay at the bottom of the car, moaning and weeping. . . .

"We each of us wrote down on a slip of paper what we thought was the best thing to do, so that we could not later accuse one another of having been the first to make a proposal which might have fatal results. We both voted for going on. . . .

"Now for the first time we realized the seriousness of our position; we felt small and solitary in the wide desert, and around us the whitened bones of dead camels testified plainly to the lack of water — to the boundless plains of the Sahara, which know no mercy. We forced our way on mile after mile at an average speed of ten miles an hour. At 2.30 a.m. we were compelled to stop by exhaustion. We drank a small glass of water and ate our dry biscuits. . . .

"*April 3.* We started at 5.30 a.m. Neither of us had much to say. The road grew worse and worse, and we had to put corrugated iron plates under the wheels, which would otherwise have sunk up to their axles in the sand. A few yards. Stop. Plates in front of the wheels. Stop. So we worked our way forward one hundred yards after another, through deep drifts of loose sand.

"At 5.30 a.m. we lost all traces of a road. Our only hope was to steer by the compass. We fastened a note 'going due north from here' to an empty petrol tin. We had only a few quarts of water left now and had driven scarcely half-way. . . .

"*April 4.* Started at 5 a.m. due north. Sand was worse than ever, if possible; water getting less. We stopped drinking. Our situation was practically hopeless. At 12.30 p.m. we came upon the old tracks again. At 1.45 a speck appeared on the horizon. It was a metal tank. Did it contain water? We put on speed. The tank was empty.

"At 3.30 a.m. we got into fearfully loose sand. The car sank into it up to the axles. We had only a little water left, and had a raging thirst. We compromised, gave the car half, raised it with the jack, and put the plates under the wheels again. Clouds of steam poured out from under the cap of the radiator. We climbed a low hill, with the greatest of difficulty, and what did we see? Was it really possible? Five cans standing out in the middle of the desert, scarcely half a mile away, as if it was the most everyday thing in the world.

"Blixen got out and went up to them. He could not walk fast; so at least it seemed to me who remained sitting in the car in the sand. I saw Blixen shake the first tin; it seemed to be full, but did it contain water or petrol? He came back with feverish haste for a spanner to get the cap off with. We used the plates again and at last stood by the vessels, which it did not take us long to open. Water! We are saved! At least we feel that we are, though we are only half-way and the endless Tanesruft desert lies before us. It took some time to bring poor Ali to life again. . . .

"The road grew better and better, and at 10.30

a.m. on April 6 we arrived at Reggan, having covered 1,880 miles from Kano. For the last 750 we had not seen a living soul."

This is, as I have said, an extract from Sir Charles Markham's diary. I myself have not much to add, except that we found the rest of the journey to Algiers a mere pleasure trip after the hardships we had endured.

Our International truck was the first car not specially built for the purpose that had forced its way across the Sahara — and the trip had, all things considered, been a success.

Though we did not really deserve it.

XX. *An Elephant Farm*

About a hundred and eighty miles from the southern boundary of the Belgian Congo lies a little place called Wando, so named after the last chief who lived and ruled there, some years ago. I knew this Wando well, and we often went elephant-hunting together. He was a hard — perhaps a little too hard — and courageous man; he admitted himself that he was perhaps a trifle strict; but there were people who called him cruel. Although he sold his ivory and lived upon what he could get for it, he loved hunting for its own sake.

If Wando was cruel, he had inherited that characteristic from his father, a man who never compromised with his principles, but went ahead ruthlessly in everything, even where his own flesh and blood were concerned. One day I saw Wando conversing intimately with a man with no hands.

"Who was that poor fellow?" I asked.

"My younger brother," Wando replied. "I'll tell you how it happened."

The fact was that Wando's brother had once cast a tender eye on a pretty young woman in his father's harem — and perhaps things had gone a little farther than amorous glances. But such a thing is *lèse-majesté* and is punishable by the cutting off of both hands. In cases that call for leniency the crime can be atoned for by the loss of only one hand, but the chief-father inquired into the affair and found that there were no extenuating circumstances. The sentence was pronounced, and — what made it even more cruel — Wando was ordered to carry out the punishment. In his father's presence, and under his supervision, the elder brother had to mutilate the younger — he cut off both his hands and checked the flow of blood with red-hot iron. But he did not, by so doing, cease to be a brother — the two were still the best friends in the world.

Whether this horrible episode had any influence on the development of Wando's character in later years I do not know, but the fact is that he became hard and cruel.

I was with him one evening when a servant was to be flogged for some trivial reason. The Belgian law lays down that no more than twelve strokes may be administered, and chiefs in the service of the State are subject to this law. When the boy had received twenty strokes I reminded Wando of the existence of the law.

Wando laughed.

"We haven't begun to count yet," he replied. "But we can begin now."

And so the poor devil got twelve more lashes.

There had been complaints about Wando's cruelty before this; the Belgian authorities had been keeping an eye on him, but had let him off with a warning, seeing that he was an able fellow, who at any rate maintained discipline among his people. But when he went so far as to begin throwing spears at his subjects for his private amusement and at the same time became more and more immoderate in his love of strong drink — which made his temper worse — it was impossible to overlook his proceedings; he was deposed and banished to another part of the country.

Once when I was hunting with Wando, just

where there is now an elephant farm, below the Belgian commandant's house, we arranged a drive, as Wando was anxious to get meat for his people. During the drive a waterbuck rushed at one of the beaters and drove his great twisted horn right through the poor fellow's stomach; he was carried a long way on the horn before the buck shook him off. I was on the spot at once, but the case was hopeless. Not a sound of complaint passed the man's lips. Luckily I had morphine enough in my medicine chest to make his last hours more or less bearable.

Yes, there was an elephant farm below the Belgian colonel's house! The story of the origin of this remarkable breeding establishment is a rather curious one. For a long time — hundreds of years — it was regarded as an axiom that the African elephant could not be tamed. When skeptics pointed to the elephants of India and Ceylon, which could be made to perform a great many useful services for man, people simply shrugged their shoulders and declared that the Indian and the African elephants were only very distantly related — till one fine day some sharp fellow pointed out that anyhow the hundred elephants Hannibal took with him across the Alps were African, and that in

AN ELEPHANT FARM

that case they had received the necessary training. That argument made an impression. The Belgians in the Congo set about the business a few decades ago, and now there is a model farm for the capture and training of elephants, just at the spot where Wando once had his headquarters.

Quite remarkable things are done there under the direction of a former Belgian cavalry officer named Offerman. This man combines a keen interest in, not to say enthusiasm for, his task with a unique power of organization. First-class discipline prevails on his farm, not only among his subordinates but also among the elephants, who are tended with the same care as racehorses in an English stable. Each elephant has its keeper, on whose shoulders the immediate responsibility rests for both its tending and its education. The period of training is twelve months, and at the end of it the pupil undergoes an examination, which he must pass with honors or God help the teacher. The elephant must be able to draw a plow and a truck, carry machine-guns and ammunition, perform a right and left about turn, stand up and lie down at a word of command, and so on — and it is very seldom that an animal fails to pass the test.

Every year about twenty-five elephants about ten years old are captured. The actual capture is, of course, most exciting and dramatic, but, thanks to the excellent organization, no loss of human life need ever be apprehended. Offerman and his chief assistants are mounted; the catchers, on the contrary, work on foot in parties of sixteen. When a herd of elephants with a sufficient number of ten-year-old beasts has been discovered, the whole flock is surrounded by natives specially called up for the purpose. Some of the older beasts are shot, as many as possible of the undesirable ones are frightened away, and the various groups of sixteen catchers select and surround their victims.

When the young elephant finds himself surrounded, he rushes to and fro, vainly endeavoring to get out. In an unguarded moment a black creeps behind the elephant, casts a stout lasso about one of his hind legs, and in a twinkling the other end of the rope is made fast to a tree. If he tries to attack a native in front of him, another lasso goes round one of his forelegs. Then his fate is sealed. The ropes are hauled in, he stands at full stretch; the sixteen rush at him from one side and throw him down. Two thicker ropes are made fast round his belly and breast; then an old trained elephant is led up, the thicker ropes are made fast to the old elephant, the ropes which keep the captive's legs bound are loosed, and the future pupil has to fol-

AN ELEPHANT FARM

low the foster-mother thus forced on him home to the farm.

They have to spend several days and nights fastened together in this fashion. The old elephant accustoms the young one to the daily routine. The young one goes out too when the old one brings in food for the night — bushes and grass tied together in large bundles. He goes out for the daily bathe in the river at two o'clock in the afternoon, and he has his own boy who lulls him to sleep every evening with rhythmical wavings of a palm-leaf whisk.

In a week he is an independent individual. He no longer needs his foster-mother, but knows exactly how the day is to be spent, and, as I have said, within a year he can place the machine-gun on his own back and, when he is harnessed to his truck, arrange the harness if any part of it is displaced. He knows when it is twelve o'clock, for then the bugler gives the signal, and the elephant hastens home to his dinner. He knows every driver and boy on the farm, for each has his special scent. I take off my hat to the Belgian Government, which has really sacrificed large sums to get this model farm in working order, and to Colonel Offerman, who will go down to posterity as a pioneer in the endeavor to place at the service of mankind the

African elephant's admirable qualities as a domestic animal.

When the talk turns on capturing wild beasts alive the name of Schultz of Arusha is bound to crop up. There is always a market for them in Europe — zoological gardens and menageries form a clientele which requires constant renewal of its stock — and Schultz sells to them all. Before the World War he was Hagenbeck's agent and was regarded as one of the few really dependable suppliers of first-class live wild beasts.

I know Schultz pretty well, and I always enjoy going to his place and looking at the beasts he has caught. A peculiar friendship exists between Schultz and his captives; in one way or another he seems to have made them feel that they can have confidence in him. They live at his place in comfortable enclosures "with all modern conveniences," and when they are transported they travel in roomy boxes, with plenty of litter. Schultz — or his son — always accompanies the beasts on their journeys to make sure that they are properly fed and looked after.

His annual turnover varies a great deal, but seldom falls below fifty zebras, antelopes, and gazelles, a few giraffes, and an odd elephant or rhinoceros. Should some animal not be in stock, Schultz does not admit defeat. Give him a few weeks and he will get what is required.

The capture of such a beast as a young rhinoceros demands not only calculation but real personal courage on the part of the man who casts the decisive lasso about legs or neck. Much of this work is done on horseback. The animal is first tired out and surrounded, and the lasso is thrown, but then a great deal of tact is required from the captor's side to make the beast understand that it has fallen into the hands of friends and not of deadly enemies. The art of capturing the animal is but a small part of the whole; the art of getting it home alive and making it survive the shock is beyond comparison the most difficult thing.

XXI. *Courage and Endurance*

THE INDIAN rajahs have from ancient times hunted the gazelle with the cheetah, or hunting leopard. This method of hunting can most nearly be compared with old-time hawking. The leopard is blinded, like the falcon, with a hood over its head till the game it is to pursue has been chosen; when the hood is removed, the animal is let loose and hunts by sight — not by scent as a dog does.

The cheetah is considered the fastest animal in the world over a short distance; a well-trained hunting leopard never misses his prey. He pursues it like the wind and finally kills it with a swift grip of its throat. It is fascinating to follow a hunt with this animal trained by nature for its special purpose for thousands of years; to see every muscle straining, the heavy tail serving as a rudder, and the gleaming, piercing eyes bent on their goal.

There are quantities of hunting leopards all over Africa. It is the only wild beast which can be said to become absolutely tame. A hunting leopard will follow you like a dog; it lies on the sofa and purrs like a cat when you come near. Unfortunately, like the leopard, it has a skin which fulfills a pretty woman's dream of a winter coat, and is, therefore, often shamefully shot. The law in some countries has forbidden the wearing of feathers in hats, but, inconsistently enough, woman is still allowed to deck herself with impunity with the skins of innocent monkeys and cheetahs.

Just because ridiculous prices have been paid for these skins during the last five years, the leopard is now threatened with complete extermination. Certainly the British game laws have at long last intervened, and it is forbidden under severe penalties to kill the leopard and trade in its skin without a special license — but I fear that this law has come too late. In any case it will be many years before the numbers of the leopard have regained normal.

The leopard, too, can give the sportsman thirsting for sensation more hair-raising moments than, perhaps, any other animal. He is fierce, cunning, courageous, and as swift as a hawk. The leopard has the unpleasant habit of hanging round houses, stealing the natives' sheep by night, looking for white men's dogs, and fearlessly entering buildings; and therefore, perhaps not quite fairly, he has got such a bad reputation that to kill him is considered a meritorious act. A leopard which night after night wandered round my house at N'gong played the chief part in one of my first hunting adventures in Africa. I could hear his steps at night, and as I had two dogs, windows as well as doors had to be shut to keep him out.

I did not know so much about the hunting of African wild beasts then as I do now, so I set up a scissors trap on the veranda and invited three of my neighbors to dinner. We had got no farther than the soup when the spring of the trap clanged outside and a furious roaring told us that the ruse had succeeded. I rushed for my rifle, but before I was out of doors the leopard, with a violent jerk, had torn the trap from the chain and disappeared into a thicket close by.

We had no choice but to leave him in peace till next morning. We succeeded in locating him by throwing stones. He had taken refuge in an absolutely impenetrable thicket full of long grass. I was young and inexperienced, and after a long conference with the blacks I asked if one of them would cut a way towards the leopard with a " panga " if I went just behind him and protected him with my rifle. After a great deal of laughter and discussion a Kikuyu boy at last stepped forward and volunteered. He cut and cut, and I stood behind with the rifle. I had no idea then how dangerous such a proceeding was; I stood there quite quietly till suddenly the leopard sprang at us with a fearful roar, trap and all. He received my bullet in the head as he leaped, and life must have been extinguished as one puts out a light. But he fell a couple of yards behind me, although he had carried with him through the air a trap weighing at least forty pounds. He was the biggest leopard I have ever seen.

Another proof of the leopard's courage comes into my mind. Two years ago I was down at Serengeti with two friends, Krister and Gunilla Aschan. We had seen two leopards going towards the bed of a river, and succeeded in gradually approaching them. One of them was actually in the riverbed, while his mate sunned herself by a tree about two hundred yards away. Krister shot the leopard in the shoulder, perhaps rather high — the beast began to jump up and down, roaring. Then it fell, but rose again and fell a second time. I knew more about the leopard's habits then than the first time, so I kept a watchful eye on the female. What I suspected happened next moment — she came tearing straight at us, tail in air, looking like a lump of gold. I was not shooting myself, so I called to Krister:

"Look out, she's coming!"

But he misunderstood me; he thought I meant the beast he had shot, and did not even look at its mate; so I had to fire at the last moment. The female leopard, with her quick eyes and intelligence, had doubtless seen at once that the danger which threatened her friend came from us; and there stood two white men with two blacks behind them, four against one. She knew we were too many for her mate, but nevertheless she came on as though fired from a gun, impelled by the best feelings in the world, a faith and loyalty reckoning nothing of death.

Talking of courage, the black man who lives all his life in dangerous regions often gives proof of the inborn loyalty I spoke of. Charles Bulpett is known all over Kenya — he hunted for many years in those parts in his great days. He still lives in

COURAGE AND ENDURANCE

Kenya, aged eighty-four, plays bridge every evening, and drives his car every day — a unique living advertisement of the climate of Kenya. One day many years ago this old gentleman was hunting lions on the Athi plain in the neighborhood of Donya Sabuk. He wounded a lion, which immediately attacked him and knocked him over, making him drop his rifle. His only companion, a Somali boy, who had no spare rifle with him, rushed up to the lion, thrust his bare arm into its jaws and let the lion chew it to pieces while Bulpett scrambled to his feet, got hold of his rifle and shot the animal.

The native, generally speaking, has endurance, but if he is put to a real test against a white man, it is usually the black who first throws up his hand. A white man has more energy and keenness. When he gets tired he goes on all the same, but a tired Negro is done for. I have often made long marches which only a few of the blacks have been able to keep up with to the finish.

The ordinary day's march with loads is about eighteen miles a day, but I have done as much as thirty-six miles in a day with trained porters. The farthest I have ever gone in a day is fifty-four miles, but only two boys out of the ten with whom I started could keep up with me. We marched practically without stopping from three in the morning till nine the same evening, and I dared not sit down, for I should most certainly have gone stiff and not been able to start again.

One's powers of endurance are often put to a severe test when out elephant-hunting. One does not, as a rule, do record distances — there are not, as a rule, any roads to follow and measure; one has to track as one goes; one is on one's legs all day, from dawn to late at night, without any rest to speak of, and this perhaps day after day. The hope that one may reach one's quarry at any moment has a marvellously stimulating effect — exertions and distance are somehow made to seem much less than they are.

Once in the heart of the Congo forest I got a telegram telling me that I must go to Europe at once. I had with me a friend named Mello, who was to go home too. We were 260 miles from the Stanley Falls, and as we had no means of finding out when a boat would leave, we decided to walk there as quickly as possible, promising our porters double pay if they improved upon the usual daily marches. We covered the 260 miles in ten days. But one goes all the time along such beautiful paths through the forest, where monkeys and birds enliven the scenery and palms and lianas relieve the monotony of the woods, that the distance does not seem so terrifying.

The monkey tribe is particularly richly represented in those parts. I myself have observed no fewer than eleven different kinds of monkeys — including the baboon, the black colobus monkey, a little brown monkey with a white nose-tip, the ordinary gray monkey along the rivers, and a little gray long-tailed monkey with a white belly, peculiarly shy, which one only sees leaping about in the tallest trees. They live on innumerable fruits and roots and are a real pleasure to the wanderer in the gloomy monotony of the forest.

XXII. *Bad Luck*

DUNMAN was a geologist. I once met him by the Athi, about 150 miles from its mouth. I was hunting elephants, and Dunman was at the moment engaged in getting an old worn-out truck across to the other coast.

"Where are you going?" I asked.

All geologists are secretive, and although we had not a white man within a hundred miles of us, he whispered to me:

"Tippu Tip's son once sent an expedition into the Galla desert, between this place and the Tana, to search for minerals. The whole expedition died of thirst but one man, who returned to Zanzibar with the sad news and a lump of coal. I've got this

BAD LUCK

man with me, and if you like we'll join forces, and share whatever we strike."

His eyes shone with love of adventure and greed for gain, but I had to refuse with thanks, and when I had helped him across the river, I went back to my work.

A year later I came to Voi from Arusha, and there I found my old friend Dunman again. He had not found any coal and seemed rather downcast. But now it was my turn. I pulled a little box out of my pocket and showed him a few shining black pieces of stone.

"Look at these," I suggested. "An old Boer from whom I bought a farm collected these and asked me to have them examined by some geologist at Nairobi."

Dunman took out his microscope, and in a few minutes the same avarice shone in his geologist's eyes as when I last met him trying to get his car across the rough water of the Athi.

"Where are you going?" he asked eagerly.

"To Nairobi. And you?"

"To Dar-es-Salaam. But," he added, "there's one first-class piece of coal among these samples, and if you'll give up your trip to Nairobi I'll give up mine to Dar-es-Salaam; we'll go back to your

Boer friend, buy his secret, and share what we can make."

The tone of his voice suggested that the secret was worth at least twenty millions. I agreed, and the very same day we drove back to my farm. The Boer, who was not averse to a friendly agreement, told us that his grandson had found the piece of coal, but that the boy had not said where he had found it. The first thing to do, therefore, was to get hold of the grandson, and the information concerning his whereabouts was a trifle obscure; the boy was elephant-hunting near Kondoa-Irangi, and it would probably be a few weeks before he came back. A few weeks! Dunman gave a coarse laugh. He could not sit patiently for a few weeks with such a prize close at hand. So we all three jumped into my car and set a course for Kondoa-Irangi.

And there we had to search. Dunman neither ate nor slept, and at last he succeeded in working me, too, up into a feverish state of avarice, which, I may say, is not a normal weakness of mine. We could talk of nothing but the damned coal — and, of course, about what we should do with all the money we were going to make. I for my part had already decided to buy an airplane and fly straight home with my millions. How much could one put

BAD LUCK

into the Sydbank on a checking account? They certainly would not pay interest on more than a few millions.

But while we talked and speculated and dreamed gilt-edged dreams, we searched for the grandson like bloodhounds. And on the third day our endeavors were crowned with success. We found him in a hunting-camp not far south of Kondoa-Irangi and took him aside.

Dunman produced the lump of coal with trembling fingers.

"My boy," said his grandfather amiably, "you must tell these gentlemen at once where you found this stone."

"That one!" the boy replied with a broad grin, "I picked that one up at Dodoma station."

Scene!

XXIII. *1914*

NEITHER I nor anyone else who lived through them will ever forget the first days of August 1914. The day before the declaration of war a few Swedes were assembled in my house — Erik von Otter, Helge Fägersköld, and Emil Holmberg, all now dead. Of course the political situation was keenly discussed. No one knew anything, and rumors of decisive naval battles in the North Sea were already in circulation. We Swedes all felt that Sweden sympathized with Germany. We discussed our position in the event of an alliance between those countries coming about and agreed that the only thing we could do was to offer our services to England, our adopted country, with the reservation

1914

that we should be freed from military service if Sweden joined Germany.

Next day Erik von Otter and I bicycled into Nairobi and reported ourselves at the recruiting office which was already open. Von Otter went into the King's African Rifles, and I myself joined a corps which had been formed by an old South African friend of mine named Bowker and bore his name, Bowker's Horse. Much time was spent in organization, unnecessary talk, ill-conceived exercises, and continued recruiting, and ten days later we were still at Nairobi.

I complained to Bowker one evening and said I should prefer to be attached to some unit which had a chance of getting to the front soon. He proposed that I should speak to Woosnam, who was the head of the Intelligence Department, and the very next day I was commissioned by him to arrange a means of communication between Delamere's headquarters and Nairobi. Of course a man in Woosnam's position had a tremendous amount to think of just then — he only gave me quite curt orders to arrange everything myself and requisition what I needed.

I went off two days later with a pleasant feeling of impending adventure and the best hopes of being able to carry out the task which had been entrusted to me. The Swedes Ture Rundgren and Nils Fjästad came with me to help me, and in a short time we had a well-organized line of communications; motor-cycles were used on the better and longer stretches of road, ordinary bicycles on the worse roads, and native runners as links where the ground was even more difficult. But the only satisfaction we got out of it was that we could guarantee the punctual arrival of letters. There was never any fighting on that front, and after three months the force there was withdrawn. Unluckily for me, Woosnam had by that time been transferred to the Palestine front, so that I had to pay out of my own pocket for the supplies I had obtained for the expedition.

In this connection I should like to mention a unique proof of Swedish endurance. One of our Boer scouts had one day been attacked by a lioness and had his leg completely slit up, though he had succeeded in killing the animal at the last moment with a revolver bullet. But swift medical help was necessary, as well as some kind of transport for the wounded man. Fjästad bicycled the 150 miles to the nearest railway station over untrodden tracks on an ordinary bicycle in the record time of twenty-four hours. A mule-cart was sent out, the

1914

injured man's life was saved, and his limb is perfectly sound today.

Delamere had got fifty South African cavalrymen as a sort of bodyguard. One day, when I was sitting in my tent attending to the mail, a man came galloping in on a horse in a lather. He reported that the Germans had begun to bombard Delamere's camp, that his captain intended to advance immediately, and asked if I would like to come too. Of course I reported myself at once to the commanding officer, but pointed out that I had left Delamere's camp the night before and that it had then consisted of one Boy Scout tent and some ten porters, besides the Masai who followed him. So there was hardly anything for the Germans — very shrewd people as a rule — to bombard. I hinted tactfully at the same time that perhaps a thunderstorm had passed over the district. But this parenthetical observation did not fall upon good soil. The captain, who had been in the Boer War, said he knew the difference between the sound of cannon and distant thunder perfectly well, and it was not worth while to make jokes of that kind. So we all fell in, the captain read a few verses from the Bible, the gin-bottle went down the ranks from mouth to mouth, the men mounted with serious expressions, and we moved off against the expected enemy in full battle formation, with patrols out on the wings and everything as it should be.

Half-way across the plain I caught sight of two natives, and as they might possibly be my messengers carrying the mail, I asked permission to ride over to them and question them. Quite right, they were my own boys, and they told me that a storm had passed over the mountains where Delamere's camp was pitched and that it had been raining hard·when they left about eight that morning.

I reported this to the captain, who nevertheless stuck obstinately to his opinion. The little troop proceeded in battle formation against the imaginary enemy, while I returned to my work at the base camp.

Kenya was severely affected by the war. The German general von Lettow-Vorbeck used the resources at his disposal freely. There was fighting here and there all along the front. Railway bridges were blown up. The British had to send for reinforcements. First an Indian contingent came, then troops from England, and the black troops of the King's African Rifles were strengthened by recruiting. Then came South African

1914

troops, horses, motor-trucks, and all kinds of other motor-vehicles. The war in East Africa raged with the same violence as on the European front. Many men were killed in battle, many died of disease, the war out there swallowed up huge sums of money — twice the cost of the Boer War, it was said — and the losses on the English side were very heavy. Although von Lettow-Vorbeck continually retired he was not defeated; he still had his best troops in Portuguese territory when peace was concluded at Versailles. I am glad to be able to say here that no one had a greater admiration for von Lettow-Vorbeck than the Englishmen who fought against him. He was hard and severe, but just.

After the troops were withdrawn from the front on which Delamere was in command I returned home, and though I was available all the time if my services should be required, I was left on my farm for the rest of the war.

XXIV. *After Twenty-three Years*

THE TWENTY-THREE years for which I have lived in Kenya have quite transformed the country. Whereas about 1913 one could obtain only scanty, incomplete accounts of the country's fertility, rainfall, and productive capacity, the immigrant can now get clear statistical information about all these things; he can ascertain free of charge what districts are most suited for growing coffee, sisal, and fruit, for general farming or stock-breeding, and there are regular markets for all the country's products.

Nairobi is not a large town according to our ideas, but considering how few inhabitants it has, it is astonishing what one can buy there. It is like carrying coals to Newcastle when a Nairobi European, farmer or townsman, imports anything he requires from Europe.

Medicine has made enormous advances. There are excellent hospitals with skillful doctors, both in private practice and the public service. There is a greater knowledge of tropical diseases; there are now cures for both sleeping sickness and leprosy, and war is waged with success on plagues of different kinds.

Cattle diseases are numerous and devastating, but there are now effective serums and other remedies against all of them, and the farmers have now good veterinary surgeons and an excellent laboratory in their service. It is hard to get the natives to report the outbreak of infectious diseases, however, among either beasts or human beings, as they are generally skeptical of the value of our modern methods.

But the thing which has effected the most thoroughgoing revolution all over Africa in recent times is flying. All business has quickened up since it has been possible to get an air-mail letter answered in a few days, and instead of spending three weeks on board a boat one can now reach any port in Europe one likes in three days. One can travel home without difficulty and for a relatively small outlay even in small private machines. There are today airports, gasoline stations, and repair shops all along the Nile and along the north coast of Africa.

When I last came home I traveled in a private airplane with a woman pilot — Mrs. Beryl Markham — and we were in London after six days' flying. It was a splendid trip over the forests and lakes of Africa, down the fertile Nile valley, over herds of elephants and antiquities from many thousands of years ago; across the Libyan deserts, through sandstorms and thunderstorms. As I am speaking of the trip, I may add that the last stage across the Mediterranean from the Sardinian port Cagliari was not particularly pleasant. We started at two p.m., and before we were half-way across Sardinia we got into a hurricane, and the clouds hung in the tree-tops. When we sighted the coast from a height of ninety feet, I asked my pilot what she meant to do.

"Well, what do you think?" she answered.

I advised her to go high up and try to get back to Cagliari. The sea lay beneath us, white with foam, and above us was nothing but threatening black clouds.

"There's too much risk of running into the mountains, and Cagliari may be hidden by clouds

AFTER TWENTY-THREE YEARS

now. I might be able to land in a field somewhere, but I shall certainly smash up the machine."

" Then let's try for Cannes! "

" O.K."

And so we flew over the surface of the foaming sea, where the clouds rode on the wave-crests. Not till we reached six thousand feet did we see the sun again, and we flew on over endless white masses of cloud. After two hours' flying we suddenly discovered a hole in the clouds and white horses on the sea far below. We planed down to the surface of the water and sighted land only twenty miles away. We had reached the coast at Saint-Raphaël, only a few miles from Cannes, where we landed at the very inferior airport in a forty-mile gale. Those were nerve-racking hours, but such a trip is much more fascinating than a voyage in a ship, with deck-chairs and stylish bars.

But, to return to Africa, the airplane is of much greater practical importance there than in Europe, where there are railways and asphalt motor-roads everywhere. Africa is one of the few countries which have been reached by air traffic before roads have been built, and in view of the enormous distances, the airplane will certainly become an economic link as well.

Not so long ago I was out hunting with two young American millionaires, Jack Simson and his friend Armour, both from Chicago. One day Jack received a telegram from his father, president of and largest shareholder in Marshall Field's world-famed giant concern, saying that he would like to come to Africa and spend a week there if I thought he could get any hunting in that space of time.

I replied with a counter-question.

"Is expense a consideration?"

On a reply being given in the negative, we discussed how, with double equipment and airplanes as means of transport, we could arrange a trip for Jack's father in such a way that, for example, we should hunt buffalo in one place one day, while a new camp was being pitched in another place for the next day's lion-hunt. When we had arrived there by air and hunted, the first camp would have been moved to a suitable place for hunting rhinoceros, and so on. The plan was accepted, and the twenty-first day after Mr. Simson had left Chicago he departed from Mombasa having killed, besides lion, buffalo, and rhinoceros, all the commoner species of gazelle and antelope!

That's hunting in Africa — 1937 style!

Index

Abdulla (gun-bearer), 40–3
Aberdare, 30, 228
Africa: game preservation in, 27–34; cost of hunting in, 32–3; safari across, 144–6; and aviation, 283
Akka, 156–61, 172
Albert, Lake, 221, 225, 227
Antelopes, 114–17
Arusha, Prince of Wales at, 178
Aschan, Gunilla, 265
Aschan, Krister, 265
Athi, R., 11, 270; game reservation, 12–13
Avakubi, 54

Bahamas, deep-sea fishing off, 229–32
Bangi, 233–4
Baringo, Lake, 217
Blixen-Finecke, Tanne von, 5, 7, 101, 178–9, 187, 198; instance of courage of, 91–2
Blue Post Hotel, 16
Bongo, 117
Bowker's Horse, 275
Buffaloes: hunting, 23, 37–44, 128–31; charge of, 41–2, 45–6; number of, 44; habits and characteristics of, 44–50; photographing, 48–50; daily life of, 51–3; tame, 53;

INDEX

lion's attack on, 92–3; riding down, 102–3
Bulpett, Charles, 266–7
Bushbuck, 117
Butiaba, 220–1, 225
Buxton, Clarence, 194

Cameroons, 173, 243
Cannibalism, 150–3
Cattle, native, of Lake Chad, 236
Chad, Lake, 233, 236–7
Chimpanzee, tame, 237–41; and pygmy, 155; and monkey, 240–1
Coal, search for, 270–3
Congo: cannibalism in, 151–2; pygmies of, 154–5
Congo, Belgian: elephant-hunting in, 54–5, 66–70; ghost elephant of, 62–6; four-tusk elephants of, 76–7; elephant farm of, 256–60
Cooper, Major A. F.: adventure of, with rhinoceros, 111–12; lion-hunting expedition of, 119 et seq.; shoots buffalo, 129–31; photographs game, 134–41
Coryndon, Sir Robert, 146
Crocodile birds, 218
Crocodiles, 217 et seq.; hippopotamus attacks, 218–19; mode of attack of, 221–2; sacred, 222–3

Delamere, Lord, 198; herd of, 215; wartime headquarters of, 275, 277, 278, 279
Digi-digi tribe, 142
Dik-dik, 117
Dinesen, Isak, see Blixen-Finecke, Tanne von
Dodoma, 187–8
Donya Sabuk, 13, 267
Duiker, 117
Dunman (geologist), 270–3

East Africa: first impressions of, 8–14; game of, 11–13, 114–18; getting labor in, 14–26; war in, 278–9; flying and, 281–4
Ekman, Lalle, 171–2
Elanairobi crater, 132–3

INDEX

Eland, 116–17; photographing, 139
Elementeita, Lake, 29
Elephants: number of, 34, 75; hunting, 54–62, 66–71, 158–9, 168–9, 174–5, 190–4, 268; native traps for, 54–5, 75; sense of, 56; havoc wrought by, 58–9; and wounded comrade, 60–2; ghost, 62–6; wrestling match between, 71–3; daily life of, 73–5; four-tusked and tuskless, 76–7; tame, 78–9; photographing, 141, 223; pygmies and, 157–9; natives steal, 171–2; meat from, 172; pygmy, 173–4; Prince of Wales photographs, 195; "repentance" shown by, 223–4; taming and training of, 256–60; capture of, 257–9
Elgon, Mount, 206
Embu, 21
Essimingor mountains, 128–9
Eyassi, Lake, 141

Fägersköld, Helge, 274
Fara Aden, 86–7
Finch-Hatton, D. G., 179–82, 189–202
Fishing, deep-sea, 226–32
Fjästad, Nils, 276
Flamingoes, 128, 133, 206
Flying, and Africa, 281–4
Fort Hall, 16–17
Fort Lamy, 237, 242; tame chimpanzee at, 238–41
Francolin, 115
Frijs, Count Mogens, 6–7

Game, 115–18; of Athi plain, 12–13; preservation of, 12–13, 27–34; photographing, 36
Game Department, 27–8, 33–5
Game Reserves, 34; Southern, 12–13, 195–7; Serengeti, 94–6; Ngorogoro, 134; by Murchison Falls, 224–5
Gao, 245–7
Gazelles, 116
George V, King, illness of, 185–8
Gnu (wildebeest), 116

iii

INDEX

Gombari district, cannibalism in, 150, 153
Gorillas, 173–4
Gray, Colonel, 97–9
Great War, in East Africa, 274 *et seq.*
Grigg, Sir Edward, 189, 198, 202
Guest, Captain Frederick, 175
Guest, Winston, 102–3
Guinea-fowl, 18, 115

Hannigan, Lake, 217
Hartebeest (kongonin), 116
Haut-Uele, 76
Hemingway, Ernest, 226, 228–32
Hemp-smoking, 167
Hippopotamus, 128, 134, 140, 217 *et seq.*; meat of, 206; attacks crocodile, 218–19; at play, 219; canoeing among, 219–20
Holmberg, Emil, 274
Hook, Raymond, 102
Horse-racing, at Kano, 244–5
Houssa tribe, 244

Hunting: buffalo-, 23, 37–45, 128–31; license for, 28–34; cost of, 32–3; organization of expedition for, 35–6; weapons for, 35–6; with camera, 36, 135–41; elephant-, 54–9, 65–71, 158–9, 168–9, 174–5; lion-, 84–91, 96, 100–1, 120 *et seq.*, 180–3; on horseback, 100–3; with aeroplanes, 284
Hyenas, 137–8

Indian Ocean, deep-sea fishing in, 226, 228
Isiolo, 144
Ivory-hunting, 29; illicit, 176–7

Jipi, 190
Julu, King, 147–9
Juma Nandi (gun-bearer), 53, 125–7, 137, 169, 173–4

Kajiado, 194
Kano, 243–5, 247
Kasigau, Mount, 190
Kater, King, 22–6

iv

INDEX

Kavirondo, Southern, 30
Kenya: coffee-growing in, 14; getting labor in, 14–26; game preservation in, 27–34; game sanctuaries in, 34; game in, 114; fishing in, 228; and the war, 278–9; modern, 280–1
Kikuyu, 31
Kilimanjaro, Mount, 11, 121
Kilindini, 10
Kinangop, 30
Kisumu, 30
Kolbe, Mr., 105–6
Kondoa-Irangi, 272–3
Kribi, 173
Kudu, 117

Lagercrantz, Carl, 169–70
Lengai mountain, 133
Leopard: hunting, 262–4; author's adventures with, 264–6
Leopard Society, 152–3
Lettow-Vorbeck, General von, 278–9
License, hunting, 28–35
Lions: tame, 80–4; hunting of, 84–91, 96, 119 et seq., 178–83; attacking buffalo, 92–3; daily life of, 93–4; and the camera, 94, 135–7, 139–40; narrow escape from, 97–9; hunting of, on horseback, 100–1; incalculable conduct of, 103–4; market value of, 107; Prince of Wales shoots, 180–3; hunting of, by Masai, 196–202; Somali boy's courage in face of, 266–7
Luck, Cardale, 205–6

MacMillan, Lady, 241
MacMillan, Sir William, 13
Mafutamingi (gun-bearer), 77
Maktau, 190
Man-Eaters of Tsavo, The (Patterson), 103
Manjara, Lake, 128
Markham, Mrs. Beryl, 282–3
Markham, Sir Charles, 145–6; motor-boat trip of, 233–7; motors across

INDEX

Sahara, 237, 242 et seq.; extracts from diary of, 248–52
Marsabit Post, 30
Masai, 205 et seq.; reserve of, 29, 30, 194–7; lion-hunt of, 197–203; customs of, 206–8, 212; beliefs of, 211; white men and, 213–16
Maungu, 190
M'bulu, 128, 141–3; tribe, 141–2, 184–5
Mediterranean, flying over, 282–3
Mello, Mr., 268
Meru, Mount, 206
Michaeli, M'bulu chief, 184–5, 188
Mombasa, 8–10, 189
Monkeys, 268–9
Moore, Captain, 182
Moshi, 121
Murchison Falls, crocodiles and hippopotamus at, 224–5
Musa (cook), 120–1

Nairobi, 13–14, 194, 203; Game Department of, 28; line of communications for, 275; present-day, 280–1
Naivasha, 101; Lake, 29, 30, 206
Nakuru, Lake, 29, 206; province, 31
Narok, 214
Natron, Lake, 206
Neil (Boer), 121, 124
N'garuka, 132
N'gong, 264
N'goro-goro, 133–4
Niamey, 245–6
Nile, R., hippopotamus and crocodiles of, 219–22, 224–5
Nile perch, 227
Northern Frontier province, 30, 31
Northey, Sir Edward, 214–15
Nyanza province, 31

Offerman, Colonel, 257, 258, 259
Okapi, 117, 156–7
Oldoway, R., 140
Oryx, 114, 129–30
Otter, Erik von, 274, 275
Owen, Tudor, 21–4, 25–6

INDEX

Paré mountains, 190
Perch, Nile, 227
Percival, Philip, 228
Photography, of wild game, 36; of lions, 94–5; 135–7, 139–40; of rhinoceros, 113–14, 195–6; of hyenas, 138; of elephants, 195
Puff adders, 170
Pygmies: Digi-digi tribe of, 142; Wambouti tribe of, 154 et seq.; compared to apes, 154–5; superstition of, 170–1

Rainey, Paul, 101
Rhinoceros: market value of, 109–10; rarity of, 110; charge of, 110–13, 140; photographing, 113–14, 195–6; charges Prince of Wales, 196; capture of, 261
Rhodesia, Northern, game in, 114
Rift valley, 128, 132, 206
Ritchie, Captain, 194–8
Roan antelope, 117
Ross, Sir Charles, 135

Rumuruti, 102, 104
Rundgren, Ture, 276

Sable antelope, 117
Sahara, motor trip across, 237, 242 et seq.; buses across, 247
Schindeler, Fritz, 101
Schultz, capture of wild beasts by, 260–1
Selangi, 194
Sendeyo (medicine-man), 214–15
Serengeti game sanctuary, 94–6
Shari, R., 233, 234
Shark, caught on line, 230–2
Simba (tracker), 165–6, 173, 176–7
Simson, Jack, 284
Sjögren, Åke, 13–14
Snakes, 170; superstitions regarding, 168–70, 211–12
Steinbuck, 117
Superstitions, 168–71

Tabankort, 248
Tana, R., 18–19; buffalo-hunting near, 37

INDEX

Tanga hills, 92
Tanganyika, game in, 114
Tick-birds, 113–14
Tiger fish, 227
Timbuktu, 247–8
Tobacco, native use of, 166–7
Topi, 116
Trout-fishing, dangers of, 228
Turkana province, 30, 31

Uasin Gishu, 30
Uaso-Nyiro, 29, 102
Ubangi, R., motor-boat trip up, 233–4
Ufiomi, Mount, 179
Uganda: elephant-hunting in, 70–1; game in, 114
Ukamba province, 31

Vanderbilt, Alfred, 228; charged by rhinoceros, 112–13; elephant-hunting with, 174–5
Vanderbilt, George, 173, 222
Victoria, Lake, fishing in, 227
Voi, 120–1, 271; district, 31, 174, 177

Wales, Prince of: on lion-hunt, 178–83; hunt prepared for, 183–4; and King's illness, 185–8; on elephant-hunt, 189–94; photographs game, 195–6; 201; and Masai lion-hunt, 197–202; malaria of, 203
Wambouti tribe, 154–5; as hunters, 156–8; fear of, 157, 161–4; appearance and characteristics of, 164; as trackers, 165–6; drug-taking by, 166–7; rain-dispelling whistles of, 170–1
Wando, elephant farm at, 256–9
Wando, King, 76–7, 253–6
Wart-hog, 102
Westerholz, Agage, 5–6
Wild pig, 117–18
Wildebeest (gnu), 116
Woosnam, 275, 276

Yakuba, Father, 248

Zebra, 115
Zinder, 245